RUAHA
NATIONAL PARK

Published in 2005 by
The Gallery Publications
P.O. Box 3181, Zanzibar.
e-mail: gallery@swahilicoast.com

©The Gallery Publications
Text by Graham Mercer
Photographs by © Javed Jafferji and Graham Mercer
Designed by Terence Fernandes
Proof Edited by Vanessa Beddoe

ISBN: 9987 667 47 3

The author and publishers have made every effort to ensure the accuracy of
the information in this   book at the time of going to press. However, they
cannot accept any responsibility for any loss, injury or inconvenience resulting from the use of information contained in this guide.

Acknowledgements
The author and photographer would like to acknowledge support received
from the Tanzanian Minister for Natural Resources and Tourism, the passion-
ately involved Rt Hon Zakia Meghji MP; the Director of Tanzania's National
Parks, Mr Gerald Bigarube (who has also been particularly helpful) and his
staff at TANAPA; James Lembeli, Public Relations Manager, Mr Mtahiko,
Chief Park Warden of Ruaha National Park, Mr Talalai (ex-Tourism officer,
Ruaha) and all other staff in Ruaha; Geoff, Vicky, Bruce and Jane Fox of the
Highland Lodge, Mufindi; Peter and Sarah Fox and staff (among them the
efficient, welcoming Danny Mvella), Ruaha River Lodge; Chris & Silvia Fox
and staff of Mwagusi Sand River Camp, Ruaha; Nicola Colangelo of Coastal
Travel, Dar, and Malcolm Ryen for the Ruaha map and staff at the Mdonya
Old River Camp, Ruaha; Charles Dobie and Brian Gardinier and staff at
Jongomero Tented Camp, Ruaha; the Harris and Fliakos families and staff at
Tandala Tented Camp, Ruaha; the Friends of Ruaha Society and their talent-
ed, endlessly patient and helpful Chairperson Sue Stolberger and partner Rob
Glen, Ruaha; the Board, CEO and staff of the International School of
Tanganyika, Dar es Salaam; Jennifer Coxell; Rhiannon Jeffries; Richard
Phillips; BK Tanna, Gloria Mawji and last but not least the author's wife
Anjum and his other "safari partners" who have shared so many memorable
times in Ruaha. One such safari partner, Barry Whittemore, contributed the
paragraphs on Ruaha's birds, for which special thanks. Also a big *asante sana*
to Kulsum, Abid and Bashira Jafferji for supporting with ideas and projects
and finally thanks to Pietro Luraschi for contributing some photographs.

**The photographer and author dedicate this book to all those who love
and protect Ruaha and its wildlife.**

RUAHA
NATIONAL PARK

Graham Mercer • Javed Jafferji

Published by
Gallery Publications

CONTENTS

Left: Quiet waters, Ruaha
Next: Cutting through the jungle with a golden track...
The Ruaha at daybreak
Next: One of Ruaha's many elephants browses among
combretum woodland
Next: Typical Ruaha Landscape
Next: Lioness guards her kill, a young giraffe
Next: Buffalo bull caked in a natural mud-pack

INTRODUCTION

I first visited Ruaha in 1978, not long after the eminent ornithologist John Williams had declared it to be East Africa's "Park of the future".

Fortunately (from a selfish point of view) John's prediction is only now beginning to come true. In the intervening years relatively few people, including myself, were privileged to enjoy what John regarded as Ruaha's "greatest charm", the fact that it was a "completely unspoiled African wilderness".

It remains unspoiled. It is still possible to drive around much of the park without seeing another vehicle for hours, sometimes days. And the phrase "unspoiled wilderness" is no romantic exaggeration; it's appropriateness becomes clear when we learn that the area of Ruaha presently developed for tourism is no greater than one third of the park's 10,300 sq km. And that the ecosystem of which Ruaha is a part is, at 45,000 sq km, larger than Denmark.

But roads to and within the park are much improved, and many visitors fly in now rather

Left: Eyeballs in the sky - the Giraffe, with its high profile, is a wonderful indicator of predators. Including photographers...

than drive. And they have, at the time of writing, the choice of one very popular lodge and four fine, well-appointed camps, and the option, denied to us in the past, of travelling in the rains, for Ruaha now has a good network of all weather tracks. Rain or shine, Ruaha is magnificent, not because of "chocolate box" landscapes or spectacular concentrations of game but in its remoteness and wild immensity. It demands involvement. In Ruaha you have to earn your game sightings or photographs; in return the park will provide you with experiences which can be truly satisfying.

Ruaha's landscapes are rugged rather than breath-taking, but you will sometimes round a bend or surmount a hill to find such a wonderful tract of wild Africa stretched across your windscreen that you half-expect a majestically moving theme tune to go with it. And here and there you will discover nooks and crannies so pleasing that you won't want to share them with anyone other than a soul-mate.

These landscapes are watered, in the south-east, by the river that gives the park its name, and in the north-west by the Mzombe, one of the Ruaha's main tributaries. Other tributaries are seasonal, superficially drying up after the rains to form some of Ruaha's most

appealing natural features, its sand-rivers. These watercourses, together with Ruaha's variety of soil types and its position as a transition zone between East Africa and the south, have helped to produce an astonishing 1,600 species of plants in the park (compared, for example, with the Selous Game Reserve, with about 850).

Amid these landscapes, comprising at least four major ecological zones, lives a vast array of animals, many, appropriately in this big land, impressive in size as well as number. They include an estimated 15/20,000 elephants and some of Africa's most imposing

antelopes, among them eland, roan, sable and greater and lesser kudu. Ruaha is the southernmost protected area in which lesser kudu are found, as is also the case with the Grants' Gazelle and the Striped Hyena. And of course there are the big cats. Bushcraft and luck are sometimes needed to find them – Ruaha is no "Africa-for-Beginners" - but when you do you'll experience a thrill more intense than you might experience on the short-grass plains.

With 526 species of birds (more than half of those found in the whole country and nearly three times more than in North America's Yellowstone National Park) Ruaha is an Aladdin's cave for serious or not-so-serious birders. And if those enthusiasts drive from Dar es Salaam, taking in other main birding locations en route (Uluguru Mountains, Mikumi and Udzungwa National Parks, Kilombero Valley, Ruaha Gorge and the Mufindi Highlands) they could return with a pretty enviable list.

If you are new to the bush or to birding, don't worry; you will find yourself in very experienced

Top: Kimilimitonga Hill, *Hyphaene* palm in foreground

hands at the lodge and camps in Ruaha. But to appreciate the bush everyone, experienced or otherwise, needs to see it with the passionate curiosity of childhood. Pablo Picasso said that at twelve he could draw like Michaelangelo, but spent the rest of his life learning to draw like a child. To get the most from Ruaha we too must reinvent ourselves. Hopefully this guide will help in that learning process.

Best Times to Visit

Almost any time is a good time to visit Ruaha. In the old days most people, especially independent travellers, would opt for the dry season, as the weather then (mid-May to mid-November) is more pleasant and predictable, with most tracks passable. Game is often easier to find, as secondary rivers and water holes dry up, forcing many animals to drink from fewer sources, with the less luxuriant vegetation increasing visibility. Also, many people find the muted browns and yellows of the dry season appealing.

But the roads leading to Ruaha and the tracks within the park have been much improved since then, and the "rainy season" no longer has such negative associations. Of course independent travellers need to be aware of the problems which rain can bring (people travelling with good safari companies or with particular camps and lodges will be in the safe hands of experienced driver/guides) but such problems are now minimal if common sense is applied, and outweighed by many advantages.

Most of Ruaha's rain falls in January for two weeks, but in February/March there is often a dry spell of three to four weeks' duration. The park then is in many ways at its best, and although

Right: Sunrise through elephant-damaged baobab

game is not always easily seen it is abundant, as are birds, butterflies and other interesting insects. Wildflowers are also at their best, and though often scattered rather than profuse, no less beautiful than flowers elsewhere. And for photographers, artists or anyone who appreciates the aesthetic, the various lights and skies and the rich greens of the rainy season bush and hills are superb. Many people now prefer to visit Ruaha in the rains, accepting the fact that game viewing (and sometimes driving) is more difficult, but finding the many compensations well worth the risks.

Getting There

Getting to Ruaha is also now straightforward. The drive from Dar, for those people with their own or hired vehicles, is an adventure in itself. It is a long (620 km.) but often attractive drive passing through Mikumi National Park, the Rubeho Mountains and the scenic Ruaha Gorge to Iringa, capital of the southern highlands. From Iringa a good track (120 km. to the park gate) heads north-west to Ruaha. The track forks 70 km. from Iringa, its main branch leading through a string of Hehe villages, the other (the "Never Ending Road" and 10 km. longer) through a lonely stretch of *Commiphora/Combretum* woodland. This type of woodland, although common within the park, is most in evidence along these approach roads, where it is home, among many other creatures, to the shy Lesser Kudu and Bushbuck, and the uncommon and handsome Crested Guinea-fowl. The tracks reunite a short distance from the park entrance.

For those visitors who have booked their safari through reputable companies the journey, by small aircraft or by vehicle, should not pose any problems.

An increasing number of people now fly in to Ruaha, often as part of a package which includes Zanzibar and perhaps Mikumi and/or Udzungwa and the remote Katavi National Parks, or the Selous Game Reserve. The lodge and camps in the park have their own aircraft or access to charter flights which operate regularly between most of these destinations; either they or any of the leading safari companies in Dar or Zanzibar (or their agents overseas) will arrange your trip, tailored to your requirements.

Left: Fish Eagles are resident in Ruaha but during the rains many migrant birds can also be seen
Below: One good reason for getting to Ruaha – the possibility of seeing leopard
Next page: The Ruaha and Chariwindi Hill from the Viewpoint

© Pietro Luraschi

HISTORY

Colonial Times

The area we know as Ruaha has always been remote, with little recorded history, though the British explorer, soldier and diplomat James Fredric Elton passed through in 1877, following, in part, the course of the Mzombe River. Elton was fiercely opposed to the slave trade, and after exploring the Zambezi and Shire Rivers in an attempt to persuade local chiefs to end the trade had headed north to return to the coast, circumnavigating Lake Nyasa on the way. He was to die, aged 37, of malaria and malnutrition in the village of Iseke, some 50 km north of the present park's northern corner.

Between 1860 and 1880, in response to threats from the Ngoni (a warlike people who had moved northwards from their Zulu homelands) more than 100 Bantu clans in the areas around present-day Iringa united under Munyigumba, and almost annihilated the interlopers. These clans became known collectively as the Hehe, a name which already existed.

Left: Agama lizard brightens up the verandah wall of a tourist banda (hut) with its be-jewelled splendour

Munyigumba was succeeded in 1880 by Mkwawa, destined to become the Hehe's most celebrated leader. Mkwawa inspired his people to more successes against the Ngoni and other enemies, including the Maasai, whose southerly expansion was successfully resisted. He eventually controlled over 36,000 sq km of territory, centred upon Kalenga (about 18 km. south of Iringa on the Ruaha track). Here, in 1887, Mkwawa built a fort with a defensive wall, 13 km. long and over 3 m. high. He named it Lipuli, "The Elephant"), set up military camps and training drills and encouraged the use of irrigation techniques to provide extra food for his people.

With colonization in the late 19th Century the Germans tried to negotiate with Mkwawa but he chose to defy them. In 1891 he ambushed and destroyed a powerful German-led expedition at Lugalo, some 25 km. east of Iringa, killing 270 German troops, mostly native askaris, and capturing arms and ammunition which enabled him to continue his resistance for three more years.

In 1894 the Germans mounted a punitive expedition under the command of Tom von Prince, who stormed Mkwawa's fort at Kalenga and defeated the Hehe after heavy fighting. 20,000 head of cattle and 13,600 kg. of gunpowder were found there. Mkwawa escaped and in spite of a huge price on his head continued harassing German troops for a further four years. While on the run Mkwawa passed through many areas including that which is now Ruaha, and legends abound about this period.

On July 19th, 1898 the Germans caught up with him at Mlambalasi. Trapped in a small rocky overhang, he first shot his

servant and then himself (in the head) rather than face the humility of the gallows. The Germans, in a macabre display of triumph, had his head cut off and sent back to Germany where it was kept for many years in a Bremen museum. Mkwawa's body was handed to his family and buried close to where he had died. The skull, with its bullet hole, was returned in 1954 by the British and handed to Mkwawa's grandson, Chief Adam Sapi, who was later Speaker of the Tanzanian Parliament for many years, and a close friend of President Nyerere. One of Nyerere's last public acts, shortly before he died, was to open the site where Mkwawa had shot himself.

Mkwawa's skull now rests in the museum at Kalenga, with

Top: Elephant family by the river bank (Note: the well-rubbed trunk of the nearby baobab)

exhibits of Hehe weaponry. Outside the museum are the graves of two of Mkwawa's descendants, Chiefs Sapi (who succeeded Mkwawa) and Adam Sapi (mentioned above).

A third grave nearby is that of the German officer Erich Maas, shot during the hand-to-hand fighting when the fort was stormed. The military-minded Hehe, incidentally, still provide many recruits for Tanzania's army.

A few years after Mkwawa's death the Germans established a large game reserve (Saba River) centred upon what is now the north-western part of Ruaha. In 1946, when Tanzania was effectively under British control, this was re-gazetted as Rungwa Game Reserve.

Post-colonial Times

In 1964 the southern section of Rungwa was given full national park status, as Ruaha, and a decade later the south-eastern sector was added to create the park as it now stands. Since then the park has been gradually developed as funds have permitted.

The 1970s and early 1980s were disastrous years for Ruaha. By 1976 its rhino had been hunted almost to extinction (it is doubtful if the remaining few survived) and by the mid-80s its elephant populations had been drastically reduced. This situation was countered by anti-poaching operations involving the park authorities and the Tanzanian Army, who combined to defeat the organized poaching gangs. Elephant numbers have since continued to increase though there is little room for complacency; poaching (for game meat as well as ivory) still takes place along Ruaha's boundaries, especially where these coincide with the course of the Ruaha and the Mzombe, where game is most vulnerable.

A new, initially less noticeable, threat had arisen in the mid-70s with the ill-advised establishment of a large, commercial rice scheme in the Usangu Plains, the main catchment area for the Ruaha River. Imperceptibly at first, the flow of water decreased. By the mid-80s, when a second large rice farm was established, it diminished more drastically. In November 1993, the river stopped flowing completely for about 3 weeks, in 1994 for 4 weeks, in 1995 for 8 weeks and so on. The situation is presently (2005) extremely serious with the river now drying completely for up to 4 months each year.

Apart from the obvious effects upon wildlife and plants the lack of water, often at peak periods for visitors, constitutes an aesthetic disaster; tourists coming to a park named after a major river expect to

see that river, not just rocks and sand, however attractive these might be. Six ministries of the Tanzanian government are said to be focusing on the problem, together with outside experts. They need to act decisively and with wisdom.

Despite the threat (to their investments as well as the park they love) a number of people have established lodges and camps in the park. The first, Ruaha River Lodge, opened in 1982, and has since been extended. A luxury tented camp, Mwagusi Sand River, opened in 1987 and in 2002 both Jongomero Camp and Mdonya Old River Camp followed. In 2003 a third tented camp, Tandala,

opened close to the Iringa-Ruaha track and just outside the park boundary. Such investments are encouraging indicators of the park's potential but there is a paradox which the National Parks Authority and the Government cannot afford to ignore; Ruaha's value is in its wildness and remoteness, and too many camps and lodges in the same area could reduce rather than promote the park's attractions. As with the water flow problem, much wisdom and restraint is going to be needed.

Top: Exposed boulders by Ruaha River Lodge
Next page: Rain in Ruaha is more a promise than a threat - it changes the park into a wonderland of green

THE BIG PICTURE
RUAHA IN CONTEXT

The Land and its Vegetation

Ruaha is situated towards the eastern edge of the central African plateau between 7° and 8° degrees south and 34° and 36° degrees east.

Its northwestern boundary is the Mzombe River, its southeastern the Ruaha, which drains out of the Usangu Flats (sometimes known as the "Buhoro Swamp"), north-east of Mbeya. The Ruaha, augmented by the Mzombe and other tributaries (sand rivers for much of the year), eventually joins the Rufiji in the Selous Game Reserve, far to the east, their combined flow emptying into the Indian Ocean at the Rufiji Delta.

Ruaha's average altitude is around 1000 m. a.s.l. though elevations vary from 750 m. in the Ruaha Valley to 1,868 m. at the summit of Ndatambulwa, above the escarpment which separates the valley from the elevated land beyond. These altitudes might seem modest by African standards but they and the other peaks and hills contribute much to the park's visual appeal.

Left: "Burning Bush Combretum"

The park is dominated in the south-west by *Miombo*, a deciduous type of woodland composed mainly of trees of the *Brachystegia* genus, found generally at a higher altitude and in areas of greater rainfall than the mixed *Commiphora/Combretum/Acacia/Adansonia* bush which, relieved here and there by grassland, occupies much of Ruaha's north-eastern sector.

This relatively low-lying bush occupies the land between the Ruaha and the escarpment, which is, on average, about 100 m. high, though much-eroded and irregular. The escarpment, an offshoot of the Great Rift Valley further west, bends towards the Ruaha on either hand, enclosing, that area of the park (about one fifth) presently used by tourists, leaving the plateau beyond, largely covered by *Miombo* and rising gradually from the escarpment, rarely visited.

This is a pity, as *Miombo* woodland can be quite attractive. And although game viewing or birding isn't always easy in such woodland it is sometimes exciting, for certain animals, such as sable antelope and Lichtenstein's hartebeeste, are often found in *Miombo*, and some of its birds rarely, if ever, stray outside it. Less fortunately, it must be admitted that the tsetse fly also likes the *Miombo*, but this shouldn't deter the more adventurous trav-

eller. New tracks are being created above the escarpment, opening up a completely new and promising area of Ruaha. They are described briefly in a later chapter.

Broadly speaking the park embraces four main ecological zones, each with its own animal and plant life and its own character. The Ruaha and its tributaries have their narrow ribbons of riverine woodland, in which fig, acacia, tamarind, *Lonchocarpus, Diospyros,* baobab and in some areas *Hypahaene* palm are well-represented. The undulating country between these water-courses and below the escarpment is largely composed of *Combretum/Terminalia* or *Commiphora* woodland, with a scattering of

Adansonia (baobabs), especially in more open areas. Baobabs are found throughout the park but are most common in the Ruaha Valley and along the Mzombe. Black cotton grassland completes this vegetative mosaic, while *Miombo* woodland (also interspersed in places with black-cotton grassland), dominates the park's southwestern region, as we have seen.

Climate

Soil types help to determine what grows where, and so does rainfall, which as one might expect is greater above the escarpment, where it averages 800 mm a year compared with 520 mm per year at the park headquarters, Msembe. The rains generally fall between November and April inclusive though they vary in timing and intensity from year to year. The coolest month is normally June with a daytime maximum of 30° C dropping to 15° C at night. Temperatures then rise until the rains begin in November or later. Throughout the following few months they can reach 40° C during the day, falling only to 25° C at night.

Top: Thunderstorm transfixes a family of zebra and transforms the landscape during the rains
Next page: Magnificent antelope, the Roan, in a magnificent setting

PEOPLE AND CULTURE

The Hehe

As explained earlier, the predominant people in the Ruaha area are the Hehe. Although many of their men are involved with the Tanzanian defence forces and many others are engaged in a variety of occupations throughout Tanzania, most still live in and around Iringa.

Like the overwhelming majority of Tanzanians they are of Bantu origin. Visitors who drive to Ruaha will pass through several Hehe villages, especially if they bypass the "Never Ending Road". These villages, particularly those close to the park boundary, are quite attractive, with huts of locally baked brick, many still thatched, and little thatched granaries, raised on small stilts, the villages set among mangos and other shade trees and interspersed by *shambas* (small farms).

The villagers grow maize and beans, sometimes raising cattle and goats, supplementing their diet through hunting and by harvesting wild honey. They also make a potent beer from maize

Left: Parakuyo girls close to Ruaha

husks, fermented in one-time oil drums and drunk during village festivals or celebrations, when ngomas (traditional Tanzanian dancing accompanied by drums and whistles) are held. The Hehe, if approached in the right way, are a welcoming people, and an invitation to see their village should be accepted.

The Parakuyo

Here and there along the track to Ruaha visitors will also see members of the Parakuyo, a former clan of the well-known Maasai whose main homelands are further to the north. The traditional reds and reddish tartans of the Maasai have been largely replaced among their Parakuyo cousins by purple, or by patterned Indonesian materials, often with purple background colours.

They will tell you that they are "Maasai" and in a sense they are right, though they differentiate between themselves and the Kisonko clan of Maasai who occupy the southern Steppe and who were once their enemies. Nevertheless the Parakuyo have maintained most Maasai traditions, including a semi-nomadic, cattle-herding lifestyle. Men and women wear beaded ornaments, with married women shaving their heads and the young men of the former "warrior grade" sporting carefully manicured hair styles.

The Datoga

Another pastoralist people who once clashed frequently with the Maasai and who are fiercely independent in their own right have begun to move into the Iringa/Ruaha area, seeking water and good grazing for their cattle. They can usually be distinguished by their strikingly simple black wraps (worn toga-fashion as with the Maasai and Parakuyo) set off by brass necklaces and bangles, their bare arms sometimes enhanced by white bands cut from plastic bottles. These people belong to a cluster of clans known collectively as Datoga, whose traditional lands lie far to the north around Mount Hanang. They are known in Swahili as "Mangati", a name they dislike.

Other People

Other ethnic groups represented in the area include the Bena and the Gogo, both Bantu. The Bena share a tradition with the Hehe that the earliest ancestors of their rulers were two brothers, but the two tribes later (1875) fought each other at Mogoda-mtitu, a battle described as "one of the bloodiest in Tanzanian history". The Hehe claimed victory but the Bena refute this. Once a warrior race they now live peacefully alongside

those other once-warlike people the Hehe, with whom, at least in some of the villages along the Iringa-Ruaha track, they seem to be integrating. The Bena grow and eat rice as well as maize.

The Gogo, whose traditional homelands are to the north around Dodoma, were a strong and staunch people who defended themselves successfully, like the Hehe, from the nineteenth century onslaughts of the Maasai. Once entirely pastoral, they later began cultivating a variety of crops including bulrush millet, sorghum and more recently maize. The Gogo in the Ruaha area, however, are usually seen herding cattle on the periphery of the Hehe/Bena villages. They are known, in their more traditional lands, to occa-sionally live in hollow baobab trees, or to bury their dead in them.

Iringa itself is remarkably cosmopolitan and multi-religious, with various Tanzanian ethnic groups living in the mainly Hehe town. Among them is a small community of Greeks and other Europeans, together with many people of Arab or Asian extraction, including Baluchis, descended from soldiers brought from what is now a province of Pakistan and brought to East Africa, in the nineteenth century, to serve as the Sultan of Zanzibar's special guard.

Top: Hehe villager by thatched granary
Next page: Baobab at sunrise

SPECIAL FEATURE
RUAHA'S
ELEPHANTS

I n 1968/70 there were an estimated 40,000 elephants in Ruaha. By 1976 the population had fallen to around 36,000 and three years later to 29,000. Despite these estimations, in 1982 a report by Dr F W Barnes of the Game Conservancy (a UK-based organization) began by saying:

"The high elephant density in Ruaha National Park is one of the most important management problems facing Tanzania's National Parks".

The author had previously concluded that over 75% of the park's elephants (18,000 animals!) would have to be culled in order to prevent wholesale destruction of certain tree species, in particular *Commiphora ugogensis, Faidherbia albida* and baobabs. The culling took place, but by ruthlessly efficient poachers rather than parks staff. By 1984 the number of elephants was down to 24,000 and by 1987 to about 9,000, perhaps falling even further to around 4,000, one tenth of the 1968/70 estimations.

"Cometh the hour, cometh the man…" Or in Ruaha's case "men". In 1987, with elephants

Left: The elephant population in Ruaha is slowly increasing

being butchered at the rate of 1,500 a year, a man called Moirana was appointed Chief Park Warden. During his decade in office he effectively curbed the worst of the ivory poaching. His outstanding efforts were rewarded by the presentation of a National Geographic "Conservationist of the Year' Award (and $25,000). In 1988 Operation Uhai ("Life"), involving specially trained Tanzanian forces, was launched, and soon cleared the park of those poachers who still operated. Ruaha's elephant population, now under the equally watchful and committed eye of Moirana's successor, Chief Park Warden Mtahiko, has since increased to somewhere between 15 and 20,000, maybe more, said to be the largest concentration in Tanzania.

Of course the biggest tuskers were prime targets for poachers, and it will be some time before such giants are seen padding, once again, across landscapes that seem to have been created for them. But more than two decades have elapsed since the worst of the poaching, and as elephants' tusks grow throughout their lives some of the survivors will now be in their forties and fifties, and carrying substantial ivory. If all goes well it will not be too long before visitors to Ruaha marvel at the enormity of some of the old bulls and their tusks; the second heaviest pair of tusks on record were taken from a poacher in Ruaha. One weighed just over 91 kg, one just under, the equivalent of walking around with two heavyweight boxers hanging from your upper jaw!).

Such great tuskers could make a visit to Ruaha all that more memorable. Meanwhile there are some pretty big elephants coming through. And equally satisfying, a large number of young ones. Elephant societies are of course matriarchal, with (as a rule) the oldest cow leading perhaps three

or four other adult or sub-adult females and two or three very young animals of both sexes. Larger groups tend to split into two or three smaller ones, though each "bond group" will spend much of its time within a mile or so of the others and will sometimes reunite, especially in times of drought.

To watch such family groups feeding among the woodland, or drinking and bathing in the Ruaha, or digging "boreholes" in one of the sand rivers, is both entertaining and satisfying. Groups of 100 or more are sometimes seen, but much smaller groups are the rule, especially when good rains allow the herds to disperse throughout the park and beyond, many seeking the peace and shade and nutritious browsing of the *Miombo* woodlands.

Whatever the size of tusks or groups, Ruaha's elephants are among its biggest assets - in more ways than one.

Top: Elephant and giraffe by the Mdonya
Next page: Elephant mothers (and sisters) are very caring and protective towards younger family members

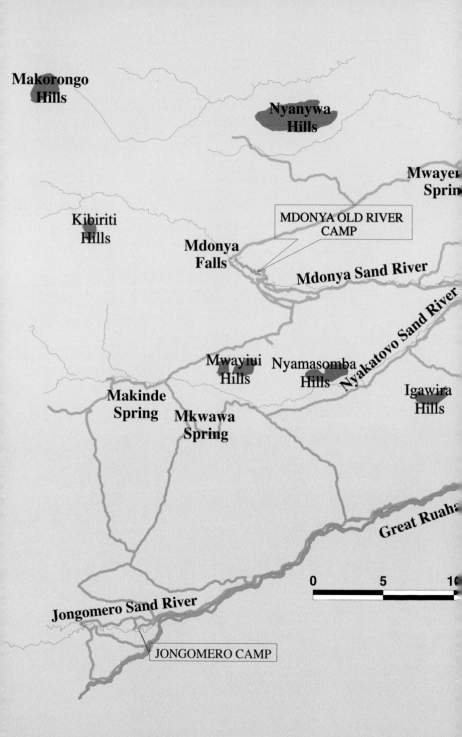

Makorongo
Hills

Nyanywa
Hills

Mwayer
Sprin

Kibiriti
Hills

MDONYA OLD RIVER
CAMP

Mdonya
Falls

Mdonya Sand River

Nyakatovo Sand River

Mwayiui
Hills

Nyamasomba
Hills

Igawira
Hills

Makinde
Spring

Mkwawa
Spring

Great Ruaha

0   5   10

Jongomero Sand River

JONGOMERO CAMP

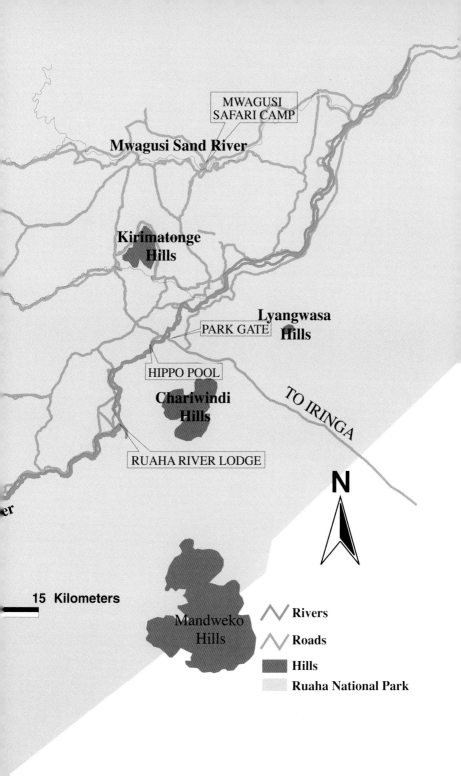

THE PARK, ITS MAIN AREAS AND WILDLIFE

Msembe

Msembe, where the park headquarters are situated, is a pleasant area, with low, undulating hills and open grassland, stubbed with baobabs and embraced by a long, gentle bend of the Ruaha, beyond which rises the 1220 m. bulk of Chariwindi ("Hill by the River"), one of Ruaha's most familiar landmarks.

The animals find Msembe pleasant also. One, the Defassa Waterbuck (*Kobus defassa*), for a particularly good reason, for waterbuck are well named, and unlike many other antelope must always be within easy reach of water. Regarded as a classic example of a territorial species the bull waterbuck will fight, occasionally to the death, to secure his territory, yet will "chivalrously" allow competitors to cross it in order to drink, should water be scarce, providing the intruder shows due deference. They are handsome animals, especially the males with their heavily ridged, upward sweeping horns. Entirely grazers except in very dry conditions, they are slightly bigger than

Left: Bull buffalo crossing the Ruaha at Msembe, under the bulk of Chariwindi

European red deer and somewhat similar in outline. Both males and the hornless females have shaggy grey to grey-brown coats with attractive white ruffs around their throats.

Another commonly seen animal around Msembe is the Black-backed Jackal (*Canis mesomelas*). To some people "cute" it is in reality a relentless killer, which in groups can kill even medium-sized antelope, tiring them out by constant harassment before eating them alive. More often they feed on smaller mammals and reptiles, carrion, birds, insects, eggs and even fruits and berries, assisted by a sense of smell 50 times more effective than our own. But the "canny" jackals have also learned to watch the skies for descending vultures, leading them to the next "free lunch". They are sometimes seen surprisingly close to lions, especially if the lions have recently killed. Their dark backs, contrasted with rufous underparts, take on a silvery appearance in certain lights.

During the rains Msembe is transformed into a radiant green, the lush grass often attracting large congregations of zebra. The taxonomy of the plains zebras is a little confused (and confusing!) but Ruaha's zebras are now listed by some as Crawshay's (*Equus quagga boehmi crawshayi*). The zebras can be a little confusing in themselves, for some have "shadow stripes" between the main ones and some don't. However, the zebras don't seem to mind, and with or without shadow stripes each zebra's markings are unique, especially in the shoulder region. Even in huge

groups their small family units, consisting of a stallion, several mares and perhaps two or three foals, recognize each other and stay in close contact. Biologists still debate the advantages of their gaudily patterned coats but it could be that in an explosive panic of zebras a predator might be distracted by the confusion of stripes. There are also theories suggesting that the stripes somehow help to reduce extreme temperatures, or deter tsetse flies. Wildlife photographers know the real answer; zebras were put on earth in anticipation of the auto-focus camera.

Talking of photographs, stop off by the self-catering bandas in Msembe, where you are allowed to get out and walk to the river's edge. You might see elephants, buffalo, giraffe or waterbuck across the Ruaha, with Chariwindi beyond. Or vervet monkeys or yellow baboons hanging optimistically around the bandas. The Vervet (*Circopithecus aethiops sabeus*) is an engaging, gregarious little monkey, greyish in colour with a greenish tinge, its black face framed by white fur. Vervets normally feed on fruit, leaves, seeds, insects, birds' eggs and sometimes small reptiles. They are often seen in the riverine woodland, foraging on the ground as well as off it, though being small and vulnerable they never stray far from the relative safety of the trees.

Yellow baboons (*Papio cynocephalus*) are less dependent on

Left: Black-backed jackal - cute-looking relentless killer...
Top: Family self-catering banda (hut) at Msembe

trees, though they roost in them at night and you will sometimes see them high in the branches by day, feeding on fruits or seeds. Their rangy build is deceptive for they are strong and armed with formidable canine teeth, especially large males, which even leopards treat with circumspection.

Like the vervets baboons, common in many areas of the park, have a complex social system and a predominantly vegetarian diet, though they will kill and eat certain young birds or mammals. Both vervets and baboons, where they come into contact with humans, can become a nuisance, begging for food or even snatching it. You are advised to keep food out of sight and reach.

About 1.5 km. from Msembe, just off the main Msembe – Park Entrance track, is another place where you are allowed to leave your vehicle to enjoy a picnic or to admire the view.

Known as "The Viewpoint", the turn-off is indicated by a marker cairn, R 12. There is a small banda (hut) at the end of the short track, situated at the edge of gentle, wooded cliffs which overlook a long bend in the Ruaha, beneath Chariwindi. You will often see crocodiles basking by the river, and a few hippo in the deeper pools. Please take care whenever you leave your vehicle here or else-

where, as potentially dangerous game can remain unseen, and surprisingly unaware of your presence.

On your way to the Viewpoint, or in other suitable areas, you might encounter two of the 526 bird species found in Ruaha, the White-headed Buffalo Weaver (*Dinemellia dinemelli*) and the Namaqua Dove (*Oena capensis*). The weavers suggest small white-and-brown parrots in form, but their most conspicuous feature is their red rump, which makes one wonder why they were not called the "Crimson-rumped Weaver". They tend to feed on the ground

in the vicinity of acacias or other thornbush, and to associate with the colourful Superb Starling (*Spreo superbus*), a bird as resplendent as its name.

Namaqua Doves are also dry country birds, petite with long, graduated tails, giving them an elegant, streamlined appearance. The male, greyish-brown in colour, has a black face, throat and chest, which the female lacks. "Long-tailed Dove" is an alternative and more appropriate name for this bird, as they have a widespread distribution and are not even confined to Africa.

The River Drive

The River Drive follows the Ruaha downstream from Msembe to the Ruaha - Mwagusi Confluence, a distance of around 20 km. It is a popular route (which in Ruaha doesn't mean crowded!), taking you through fine, open country, where tsetses are less numerous and where lions, and many other animals and birds, are often found. From Msembe the track heads through low hills covered by *Combretum/*

Top: Crocodile gapes to help cool itself in the afternoon sun
Next page: Yellow baboon enjoying the view, Msembe

Commiphora woodland before winding down towards the river.

Along the Ruaha you will see characteristic riverine woodland or "gallery forest". Among its species are winterthorn, figs, tamarind, acacia and the occasional baobab. The piquant fruits of the tamarind (*Tamarindus indica*) are used in Indian cooking and are equally valued by many herbivores, while certain figs are cherished, among other creatures, by fruit bats and various birds.

The fruits of the "Winterthorn" (*Faidherbia albida*) are coiled like apple parings and when ripe are gloriously golden or russet, as if oven-baked. They too are relished by many herbivores, not least elephants, which will shake the *albida* vigorously to release the fruits, which they polish off one by one with the addictive eagerness of humans eating crisps. Rather risky crisps in this case, as they sometimes contain cyanide, but wild herbivores don't seem to mind and the pods yield 15% crude protein. Prior to the dry season, before they break into new leaf, the albida live up to their "Winterthorn" epithet, their silvery branchlets adorned with drifts of pale-cream blossom.

Among the first trees you encounter, however, soon after descending to the river, are *Acacia tortilis*, the archetypal "umbrella thorn" of the East African savannah, though they are not widespread in southern Tanzania. Their fruits are contorted into "apple-rings" like those of the *albida*, and similarly sought after by many game animals, but are much narrower in form. Like all acacias the *tortilis* is armed with thorns, the *tortilis* having two types, one short and hooked, one long and straight. This duality of thorns and its distinctive fruits make the *tortilis* easy to identify. Incidentally it was from the timber of this tree that Noah built his ark, so if you get caught in a downpour you know where to go – you'll have plenty of animal passengers...

Including lions, though these are not as easily seen in Ruaha as in the short-grass plains of some of the northern parks. They are regularly encountered, nevertheless, especially along the rivers and sand rivers. They will hunt at any time if the opportunity arises but generally flop and rest once the sun's heat becomes uncomfortable. In this mode they look as docile as labradors but don't be deceived. They are killers, on standby. Even when resting, their massive shoulders and forelegs, contrasted with the relatively light and (when seen

Right: Grimacing lion shows his formidable teeth - and his "sand-paper" tongue, which can rasp the skin from a kill

end-on) surprisingly slender body and hindquarters, reveal a lethal combination of power and agility.

Lionesses reach two-thirds of their adult size by the age of two, whereas males are rarely fully grown even at four. This faster development in females may reflect the fact that they do most of the hunting and need to be as powerful as possible as soon as possible, though males, which spend much of their lives alone or with other males, are quite able to look after themselves.

Having a large mane cannot help during a stalk, but many males in the southern parks have very scanty manes, probably an adaptation to the thicker bush and warmer climate in the south, as opposed to the cool, open plains of the Serengeti and Ngorongoro.

If you do see lions hunting, it is best to watch from a distance, at least initially. Too close an approach will alert the lions' intended prey and spoil the hunt. More often than not the lions spoil the hunt for themselves; time and again they can be within a few metres of an unsuspecting zebra

buffalo more often than they would probably choose, for a full grown buffalo weighs four times as much as a lion and three times more than a wildebeest. And unlike the wildebeest, which gives up with little more than a resigned grunt, the buffalo does "not go gentle into this goodnight". Once killed, however, a buffalo provides enough meat for a whole pride.

Lions are the only members of the cat family which are sexually dimorphic (different in appearance) and the only felines with tufts at the end of their tails. You will also notice that the pupils of their eyes are circular, like all big cats but none of the smaller ones. What lions do have in common with other cats is the need, in the female, for repeated sex, to stimulate ovulation. One male in the Serengeti mated 145 times within 55 hours with one lioness, and 12 times with another. Mating takes only about twenty seconds as a rule but even so, weary dominant males sometimes give way to an eagerly waiting subordinate, with no obvious jealousy. And perhaps much relief.

You should certainly see, along particular reaches of the river, buf-

or antelope and fail to kill it. But any animal that can afford to spend 20 hours or so out of 24 resting or mating can hardly be accused of inefficiency. Lions, like all cats, rarely exert themselves unnecessarily.

In Ruaha, they have to exert themselves rather more than in certain other parks, because of the rugged nature of the terrain, the wide dispersal of prey species and the absence of wildebeeste, much favoured by lions elsewhere, and relatively easy to catch and subdue. Lions in Ruaha are forced to hunt

Left: Waiting for Mum to return from the supermarket
Next page: Lioness and family in fine condition (note the slender body, from in front or behind, of the lioness)

falo coming down to drink, or hippo and crocodiles wallowing or basking, as well as a number of other animals.

And many birds, especially waterfowl such as Spurwing and Egyptian geese, a variety of herons, egrets and storks, white-headed plovers and several waders, particularly during the months of the northern winter, when Ruaha's abundance of birds is augmented by migrants.

One intra-African migrant you might see, if you are lucky, is the African Skimmer, a superficially tern-like bird, dark above and white below. The skimmer has a most unusual bill, red with a yellow tip and very slender in vertical section. Its lower mandible projects some 2.5 cm. beyond the upper and when feeding the birds skim the surface of the river, ploughing the water for unsuspecting fish with its extended lower mandible.

Skimmers are usually crepuscular (twilight) feeders but are apparently active on moonlit nights, taking fish up to 8 cm. long. Interestingly, they do not lift their bills when a fish is caught, but lower their heads and snap the bill shut. How conscious they are of the presence of obstacles is unknown, but flying by twilight and at speed over African rivers, often minefields of natural debris

and submerged rocks, with two thirds of your lower mandible under water, must be a precarious way to make a living.

You will also see various birds along the river bank. Helmeted Guinea-fowl (*Numida meleagris*) are numerous here in the dusty open areas that they love, and so are Von der Decken's Hornbills (*Tokus dekeni*) which along with other hornbill species nest in holes in trees, often baobabs, the female being "walled in" by the male using a muddy, cement-like material. She remains imprisoned until the chicks are hatched and strong, undergoing a complete moult in

the meantime. During this period the male feeds her through a small aperture left for the purpose. Eventually the female breaks out but the nest and young are immediately sealed in again, both parents now sharing feeding duties until the chicks peck their way to freedom.

The Red-billed Hornbill that is also plentiful here, as in many other areas, has recently been discovered to be a new species. Formerly listed as *Tokus erythrorhynchus*, it has now become *Tokus ruahae*, the Ruaha Red-billed Hornbill. It has black eye-skin rather than pink, and a pale eye.

Although the river and its environs are the main focus on this drive, don't neglect the bushed grassland which sweeps down from the west, for a less ambiguous bird, the Ostrich (*Struthio camelus*), is sometimes seen here. The cocks are easily picked out by their predominantly black plumage, their small harems of hens less obvious in grey-brown. Their specific name means "camel-like", an unlikely comparison but not inappropriate, for the

Below: Trial of strength
Next page: Zebra by the River Drive during the rains

Ostrich is a most unlikely bird. The largest living one, it can run at 70 km. per hour and is capable of maiming or even killing a lion with a single kick. The male is also unique among birds in his possession of a penis. As you might discover if fortunate enough to see the intricate mating display of these birds, in which a receptive female engages in an elaborate "dance", repeatedly ducking and ruffling her otherwise redundant wings before crouching to allow the cock to mount.

The cock will mate with several females which later lay between 15 – 50 eggs in one communal nest, a simple scrape in the ground made by the cock. Nesting duties are segregated, the male sitting at night, when his dark plumage is far less noticeable, the duller female by day. Eggs take over 40 days to hatch and contain the equivalent of about 24 chicken eggs. Don't be tempted, should you find one, to take it back for breakfast, as apart from breaking park regulations it will take two hours to boil…

In this same open area you will sometimes see Grant's gazelle, *(Gazella granti)* the only gazelle found in Ruaha. It is also found north of the Mwagusi, though its occurrence close to water is coincidental, as the gazelles don't need to drink, obtaining moisture from the grasses and leaves that make up their diet. Both sexes carry horns, though the male's are much longer. The gazelle is one of the prime prey species of the cheetah, which although not abundant in Ruaha is regularly seen, sometimes in this grassland.

The Mwagusi

From the end of the River Drive at Marker R 24, where the Ruaha is joined by the Mwagusi, you can drive to the Mwagusi Causeway along the river's southern bank, a distance of about 12 km. Not that you see much of the Mwagusi on the way, just tantalizing glimpses through its screen of trees and bush, but sand rivers (as the Mwagusi often is) always inspire expectation.

The first glimpses one gets when heading west from the Confluence are of the Mwagusi at its broadest, as it runs its final course into the Ruaha. When it is bereft of surface water you will often see giraffe, zebras and elephant here, out on the open sand.

The country through which you now pass is of a somewhat indeterminate nature, where coarse grasslands and scrub decline gently towards the Mwagusi, bordered in this area by stands of "vegetable ivory" palm, which adorn many reaches of the Mwagusi and other water courses.

These unbranched palms, *Hyphaene ventricosa*, can grow to 18m. and like most palms possess an exotic grace. Their pear-shaped nuts, about 5 cm. in diameter, are orange-red to dark brown and produced in huge quantities, much to the delight of elephants and

---

Left: Female impala test the breeze
Top: Exotic Hyphaene palms along the Mwagusi

baboons. And to many human beings outside the park, who make a mildly intoxicating wine from the sap, often distilled into a highly potent spirit. Fronds from the emergent palms are used for making woven mats and baskets.

The seeds of the fruits are covered by a spongy, fibrous pulp which has a sweet, gingery taste, giving rise to one of the tree's common names, the "Gingerbread Palm". The endosperm at the core of the seed is white and hard, resembling vegetable ivory (hence the palm's other common title). It is carved, in Namibia and West Africa, into tiny "ivory" trinkets.

Further along the Mwagusi you pass through its attendant woodland and in places *Terminalia* thicket, and at one point a lovely, extensive grove of baobabs, eventually emerging close to the Mwagusi Causeway. The main sand river here is just north of the causeway, and again lined with vegetable ivory palm. In the neighbourhood of the causeway and the Mwagusi Sand River Camp just beyond you might see a family of greater kudu, consisting of a small group of females and young, sometimes,

especially in the early dry season, with the adult male in attendance, though bulls often roam in all-male groups. The Greater Kudu (*Tragelaphus strepsciceros*) is one of the most imposing of antelopes, adult bulls sometimes 1.5 m. at the shoulder, their handsome necks and heads surmounted by beautifully spiralling horns.

Despite their size greater kudu, their grey or grey-brown coats broken by seven to ten white stripes, are well camouflaged amid the bush or woodland which they frequent. So much so that they often survive, outside the park, close to settlements. In Ruaha, where people rarely represent a threat, they can often be observed at close quarters, though mature bulls are more wary than females. Greater kudu are among the gourmets of the bush, browsing on a wide range of leaves, herbs, fallen fruits, vines, tubers, succulents and flowers, including, in the dry season, the scarlet "toothbrush" flowers of the *Combretum paniculatum*.

This *Combretum*, common in many parts of Ruaha and often known as the "Burning Bush", adds its lovely sprays of colour to the generally muted tones of the dry season, not only through its profusion of bright red flowers but also through a similar profusion of predominantly pink, five-flanged seedpods, decorating the branches like tiny Chinese lanterns.

From the causeway a track leads south, completing a circuit should you wish to do so. It passes, as do many elephants and other game animals, through a mosaic of woodland and patches of wooded grassland, before descending through the gentle, more open hills which surround Msembe. But we will continue along the Mwagusi west of the causeway, via

Left: Well-worn baobabs, rubbed by generations of elephants

an area known as Mbagi, and on towards the escarpment.

This is another important game area. When the river is dry it is possible to drive across the sand, at certain points, to the northern bank, though anyone unused to driving in the bush should proceed with caution, following the tracks of previous vehicles. In any case there is much to look for on either side of the river, and some lovely stopping places here and there where you can, if regulations permit, leave your vehicle and take a break by the Mwagusi. As always be alert for potentially dangerous game.

Large prides of lion are sometimes seen along the Mwagusi but it is pleasant, at times, to do what they often do, and relax under a shady tree. If you keep a low pro-file zebra or giraffe might come down to drink, from the braided streams that remain before the river dries up or, if already dry, from "bore holes" created by elephant. Sometimes you will see elephants digging such holes, initially with their forefeet and then with their trunks. This method of accessing the water table is made possible by natural subterranean "dams" of granite, behind which water collects close to the surface.

The African Elephant (*Loxodonta africana*) can usually be seen in some numbers throughout Ruaha, though many disperse into the *Miombo* and elsewhere during the rains. The largest aggregations are seen between January and March (another good reason to visit Ruaha at this time) when mating (of the elephants, not neces-

sarily the visitors) is at an annual peak. The act of mating, though rarely seen by human observers, is interesting in itself, as the female's vulva is situated well forward of the usual mammalian position, ensuring that for elephants, size really does matter. Fortunately evolution has equipped the male with a penis in proportion to the problem and which, when fully erect, flexes into an elongated "S" shape to enable penetration. Despite (or because of?) all this, mating often takes less than a minute.

The social life of the elephant, perhaps the world's most versatile herbivore, is now pretty well known. One facet, however, still preoccupies researchers, the ability of elephants to communicate through infrasonic sounds, too low for us to hear. Such sounds bounce off "sonic ceilings" in the atmosphere, where two contrasting temperature layers meet, enabling them to be heard by other elephants at great distances; some observations suggest 40 km, though more research on this fascinating phenomenon, only discovered in 1987, is needed. This might explain why elephants, from time to time, are seen to become agitated for no apparent reason.

It might also help to explain

Left: Lions, teaching us how to "chill out", despite the heat...
Top: Elephants - the great communicators - walk through the park in deceptive silence
Next page: Body language, elephant style

how a cow on heat for only two to three days in four years can attract the largest bulls, who wander throughout the park and its adjacent protected areas for thousands of kilometres. Scientists have recently discovered that elephants not only pick up infrasonic sounds by ear but also through their padded feet, via embedded sensors. So the "love song" of the female, unheard by us but presumably music to the ears of an adult male, is also, perhaps, music to his feet...

In the dry season September is the best month to observe elephants, though even then, when they stay relatively close to permanent water, you rarely see more than a small fraction of those present. What you will see are obvious signs of their passage (in more ways than one, for their droppings are proportional to the diameter of their intestines, and therefore good indicators of the size of the elephants themselves). You will also see, especially during prolonged drought, evidence of tree damage, as elephants tear strips off certain species to obtain moisture or nutrients, or break branches or trees to get at leaves and fruits.

Here and there along the Mwagusi, as elsewhere, you will come across the Candelabra Tree, *Euphorbia ingens*, with its tight clus-ter of upward curving "candles", fleshy, crenellated bright-green branches. The latex of this attractive *euphorbia* is quite poisonous; more than one rural African, it is rumoured, has been done away with by the addition of its dried and powdered latex to his beer. Yet rhino apparently relish the plant. You will occasionally see these *euphorbia* growing from a niche high in a baobab, where they have been "planted", presumably by birds.

Away from the river valley you will see many species of *Commiphora*, recognizable by their shiny grey bark and superficial resemblance to neglected apple trees. Most *Commiphora* produce aromatic resins (one of them myrhh, of Biblical fame, though not in Ruaha). The most common species in Ruaha is *C. ugogensis*, found throughout the park below the escarpment. These tall, yellowish-looking trees, like those of the *Miombo* woodland, remain leafless throughout most of the dry season but anticipate the rains by putting out new leaves while the land is still dessicated by drought.

Other *Commiphora* common in Ruaha include the blue bark, *C. caerulea*, easily identified by its smooth, milky-blue bark which peels freely in yellowish, papery patches, and *C. africana*. *Africana* is a shrubby, spinescent species

which also has a succulent-like bark, grey-green in colour and which exudes a pale, fragrant gum if damaged. It is known in southern Africa as the "Poison grub Commiphora", as the larva of the Diamphidia beetle, from which bushmen make arrow poison, feeds exclusively on these trees. The tree has various medicinal uses, including one used in cases of snake bite, and the resin, mixed with sheep's fat, is one of rural Africa's answers to roll-on deodorant.

Birds as well as trees are abundant along the Mwagusi, among them the Little Bee-eater (*Merops pusillus*), seldom seen far from water. One of a family noted for beauty, and of which 8 are represented in the park, the Little is probably the most numerous and the smallest. Predominantly green,

its yellow throat is set off by a triangular black gorget and a black eye-stripe. The gorget seems to "leak" into the upper sides of the breast like a water colour painting, into patches of chestnut brown, fading into lime-washed buff. Little Bee-eaters typically perch close to the ground, scanning around for small flying insects, mostly bees or wasps. They take other flying insects including, you will be pleased to hear, tsetse flies. Most insects are caught within a few metres of the perch, with a one-third success rate, resulting in about 12 "kills" an hour.

Lunda

This area, centred upon a ranger post towards the eastern

Top: Elephants need to drink regularly, partly because they have large brains, even relative to their size

corner of the park, was little visited until recent years. It can be reached by travelling downstream from Mwagusi Causeway along the northern bank of the Mwagusi, and in the dry season from the Mwagusi/Ruaha confluence. It is a little over 40 km. from the causeway, a fairly long return journey, but there are one or two pleasant stopping places along the river and of course you can turn back at any point.

If travelling from the causeway you pass through open bush country, much of it *Combretum*, roughly following the path of the Mwagusi and crossing two or three minor watercourses en route. To the north of this track the land rises in gentle contours. There are swathes of open grassland here and there, with occasional baobabs.

Beyond the Mwagusi/Ruaha confluence the track basically follows the northern bank of the Ruaha, with at least one loop road traversing a riverside terrace. Such loops, where they occur, are worth investigating, as lions sometimes lie up in them. Another detour crosses fairly open country between the river and the bush to the north, passing through dense thickets of wild lavender.

Throughout the drive you are likely to see a wide variety of animals and birds but many people go to Lunda in the hope of seeing

two of Africa's largest and most magnificent antelopes, the roan and the sable. Especially the sable, which is more at home in the *Miombo* above the escarpment, and from which it probably wanders only in search of water at certain seasons, or the short grasses on which, as a specialized grazer, it fastidiously feeds.

In a study conducted in Zimbabwe the Sable (*Hippotragus niger*) was never found more than 1 km. from water, and almost all its food was in the form of grass between 4 and 14 cm. in height. The extent of such restrictions in Ruaha is unknown, but it seems likely that the sable's heavy dependence upon water and its fairly circumscribed diet might explain its limited success as a species. What the sable does have in abundance is aristocratic glamour; the male's glistening black coat a dramatic foil to its white facial markings and underparts, its noble form crowned with great, crescentic, backward-sweeping horns, the female equally splendid in a coat of glossy chestnut but with smaller horns.

If you don't see sable or roan there are consolations, provided by the river itself and the idyllic lit-

Left: Female Greater Kudu among combretum
Next page: Storks feeding as sun rises over the Ruaha

tle spots, here and there, where you can stop and enjoy the view and the tranquility. One such spot, some 15 km. or so before the ranger post, is a little shelf of land alongside the Ruaha, perfect for a picnic. The hippos that often enjoy the river pools here will probably move out as you move in, but the scenery itself, with the little, tree-shaded terrace and the boulders and pools and tall sedges of the river, is reason enough to break your journey.

One creature which won't move out, assuming it is there to start with, is the almost ubiquitous Ashy Starling (*Cosmopsarus unicolour*). The starlings have long, graduated tails and are almost identical to the only other member of their genus, the Golden-breasted Starling (*C. regius*), except in colour. It is fascinating why two similar starlings should develop such dramatically different colouration, for the Golden-breasted, which doesn't occur in Ruaha or in fact overlap anywhere with its less splendid cousin, is as brilliant as the Ashy is dull. Ashy starlings, common as they are in the park, are not found outside Tanzania.

On the way to Lunda, as elsewhere, you might come across one or more of Ruaha's six species of mongoose. Three of them, the Egyptian (*Herpestes ichneumon*), the White-tailed (*Ichneumia albicauda*)

and the rarely seen Marsh (*Atilax paludinosus*) are mainly nocturnal, though the Egyptian, largest of all African mongooses, is much less so than the other two. The remaining three species are largely diurnal and more likely to be encountered. The Slender is characteristically seen as it dashes across the track, its long, black-tipped tail curled into a careless question mark. The Banded (*Mungos mungo*) and the Dwarf (*Helogale parvula*) are gregarious, the former often seen foraging in large groups, the latter racing for cover towards an old termite mound, from the passages of which they might peep out in communal curiosity. Dwarf mongooses have an interesting social system, as with wild dogs and certain other creatures, headed by an alpha male and female, the rest of the group having varying roles such as "nannies", hunter/foragers and look-outs. Sadly, in the event of the alpha male mongoose losing interest in the alpha female she often starves to death, despite the best efforts of other family members to clean, feed and protect her; who knows - maybe even mongooses die of broken hearts? More certainly, all mongooses are largely carnivorous, eating a wide variety of small creatures, though confrontations with snakes, while they do occur, have perhaps been exaggerated.

Another carnivore often seen along the river is the highly acquatic Nile Monitor (*Varanus niloticus*), described by one authority on exotic pets as "the toughest lizards you could ever try to tame". As they are related to the famous Komodo Dragon, largest lizard on earth (they themselves occasionally grow to be up to 2 m. long) and are said to have "a highly strung disposition" the task of taming one would indeed seem to be challenging. One might ask why anyone would want to.

Left: Banded mongoose moves in to fill the frame

Monitors are, perhaps, the nearest thing you will see in Ruaha to a dragon or a dinosaur, equipped "with teeth and jaws designed to separate flesh from bone". Actually as they grow their sharp teeth are replaced by broader, blunter ones, probably as their diet changes to include molluscs and other well-armoured prey. It is said that they will eat "anything that fits into their mouths". This certainly includes carrion, and monitors will feed from lion kills if the chance occurs. They also have a whip of a tail; even a small monitor can mark you for a week with one lash, but you have nothing to fear if you leave them alone. And much to gain, for they are among Ruaha's most interesting animals.

The related Savannah Monitor (*Varanus exanthematicus*) is somewhat smaller and less aggressive than the Nile, and found, as its name suggests, in the bush rather than by the river. It is predominantly a dull sandy brown with pale spots, but its appetite is as voracious and catholic as that of its green and yellow cousin ("these guys are bottomless pits and will eat anything that moves"). In the Ruaha dry season they can sometimes be found aestivating in trees but as the rains set in, towards or around the New Year, they begin to stir and are often encountered on the tracks. Which might explain their Swahili name, *Panga Mwaka* – "To start a new year".

Kimilimitonge

Kimilimitonge, far from Lunda and quite different, has one thing in common; you often have it to yourself. This rocky hill, 1158 metres high, dominates the Mbagi-Mwagusi Causeway-Msembe triangle. "*Mitonge*" means "ball of ugali" (maize porridge), "*Kimili*" being the sauce that goes with it. Legend has it that the Hehe Chief Mkwawa is said to have rested here to eat such meals when being hunted by the Germans. Kimilimitonge is worth a small detour, for the triangle of land it overlooks is often rewarding game country, and the hill is interesting in itself.

If approached from the Mwagusi Causeway via Mbagi (ie south from marker cairns W7 and W8) the route takes you through a belt of *Combretum*, including *C. paniculata*. And this is as good a place as any to confront the issue of tsetse flies (*Glossina spp*), which are common in certain areas of Ruaha, especially in *Combretum* woodland or other thick bush, and in the *Miombo*. There are several species of tsetse, one of which, *G. mortisans*, is more aggressive than the others. Bites from all tsetses can make you wince at times but visitors to Ruaha will usually only experience minor discomfort, as the flies in the park, though they are capable of transmitting sleeping sickness (Trypanosomiasis), to domestic stock, pose no serious threat to humans. All tsetse are attracted by movement, smell and colour to different degrees, with the *mortisans* species being particularly attracted by movement. Typically odour attracts flies from a distance, after which they home in on movement and colour. Apparently royal blue is their favourite colour, while black (which perhaps resembles the shade in which they normally rest) stimulates them to land. On you.

You will soon get to recognize the sickly-grey creatures, slightly smaller than house-flies, and develop strategies for dealing with them. In fact it seems that healthy adult tsetses aren't all that fond of us. Most of the flies which tap into our circulatory system are recently emerged, lacking the energy to find something better, or adult tsetses wearied by life's daily grind. Tsetse fly larvae are deposited by the mother in friable soil where they pupate. The emergent flies immediately seek a convenient host (both sexes, unlike mosquitoes, feed exclusively on blood), with the poor warthog topping the tsetse popularity charts, despite the fact that royal blue warthogs are something of a rarity. The good news is that tsetses only feed every two or three days and die young (14 weeks (females) and 6 weeks (males)). Remember too that where you get tsetses you get game; what you lose in blood you often gain in game-viewing.

Left: Highly aquatic (and highly strung?) monitor lizard

One of their hosts in this *Combretum* woodland is the Greater Kudu, discussed above, but another is its smaller cousin the Lesser Kudu (*Tragelaphus imberbis*), to many people even more attractive. Lesser kudu, at first glance very similar to their larger counterparts, have noticeable differences, other than size, including the lack of a beard in the male (hence the specific name) and more body stripes (11 – 15). Both sexes have these distinctive stripes.

There are also white, crescentic "slashes" on the upper and lower neck and a white chevron between the eyes. Males tend to be bluish-grey or greyish-brown, females and young a more reddish brown. You need to be quick to see all this, and quicker to photograph it, for they are notoriously shy.

A much smaller antelope lives among the rocks of Kimilimi-tonge itself, that "ballerina of the bush" the Klipspringer (*Oreotragus oreotragus*). Known as "*mbuzi mawe*"

hooves together, balancing on their rather rubbery tips – hence "ballerina". In the East African race females as well as males have short, spiky horns.

Klipspringers need to be agile, for Verreaux's Eagle (*Aquila verreauxii*) often patrols Kimilimitonge, and though hyrax make up about 90% of its prey the eagle is not averse to small antelopes. Described by Leslie Brown, pioneer of raptor studies in East Africa, as "the finest of the genus Aquila", this magnificent eagle is thought to hunt co-operatively on occasions, one bird flying over a hyrax colony while the other swoops down rather unsportingly from another direction. They are born to murder; the female Verreaux's lays two eggs in a precariously placed nest high on the cliffs, and within three days of hatching the larger of the two young birds heaves his brother (or sister) over the edge into eternity; Cain and Abel re-visited. In flight the mature Verreaux's, predominantly black, can be identified by the conspicuous whitish patches at the base of its flight feathers.

The Rock Hyrax (*Procavia capensis*) on which the eagle largely dines is hunted by many other animals. Even its urine is sought after

("goat of the rocks") in Swahili, and "this darling little antelope" by the Victorian hunter Gordon Cumming, the klipspringer lives up to all its nicknames. A little over half a metre high at the shoulder, and generally olive-yellow in colour, flecked with grey (the hairs, incidentally, are hollow), it is the only antelope adapted to a mountainous habitat. Its agility among the rocks is astonishing, and it can sometimes be seen perched on a sharp pinnacle,

Left: "Ballerina of the bush", the tiny klipspringer

by certain African hunters, who scrape the sun-dried, orange-coloured deposits from the rocks, mixing them with products from wild honeysuckle and wild sisal to make gunpowder. The hunters' womenfolk use the powdered urine to make lipstick. If all this seems unlikely, it is worth noting that hyrax urine ("dassiepiss") was once used in Europe to cure hysteria. Not very successfully, according to a Leyden University professor, who lamented that his patients (hardly surprisingly) remained hysterical but "rifted right well".

UPSTREAM RUAHA

Hippo Pool

Earlier we followed the Ruaha downstream from Msembe. Upstream Ruaha is in many ways different. The animals, birds and trees found on the River Drive are also found upstream, but the river changes character, its bed generally narrower and less sandy, and in places cluttered with boulders. When water levels are low these great, smoothly shaped boulders are revealed, a fantastic sculpture garden in the sand, populated by thousands of Henry Moore abstracts.

Before setting off along the main track upstream, we can visit the hippo pool just upriver of the bridge at Ibuguziwa (in effect the park entrance). The pool is alongside the river's northern bank, a short drive from marker cairn R8. On arrival you can leave your vehicle and sit on the bank overlooking the pool, a natural feature of the Ruaha. Descend the bank carefully, as this stretch of water and its sandbanks there are popular with crocodiles, which are far more wary than hippos. There are sometimes interesting birds here also, such as Night Herons.

Nile Crocodiles (*Crocodylus nilotica*), like hippos, are found along the Ruaha and other watercourses wherever conditions are suitable, and seem to be increasing. They can grow to more than 6 m, though such giants are unlikely in Ruaha. Crocodiles have a fearsome

reputation, and an estimated 200 Africans are killed by them each year. Certainly you shouldn't take them for granted, for they can move with surprising speed, on land or from water, but if you avoid the water's edge and any bordering vegetation you will be quite safe. Generally they will move out of your way quickly, making for the security of the water.

Baby crocodiles eat insects and tiny fish, moving on to crustaceans and larger fish, whereas adults, while still heavily dependent upon fish, are capable of killing a great variety of mammals or birds, large or small. Hunting techniques include simple rushes at unsuspecting victims, scything down prey with their tail or leaping from the shallows, dragging their victim into the water and drowning it. In hard times they can go without food for perhaps as long as a year.

Often unable to anchor their kill in the water, crocodiles will grip part of the animal in their jaws and roll over and over lengthwise until a chunk of meat is twisted off. They then flip the meat into the air and catch it, if necessary again and again, until the meat is lodged well down their gullet. Interestingly enough their jaws which can exert many tonnes of pressure when gripping, are controlled by surprisingly weak mus-

Below: Sinister product of 65 million years of evolution

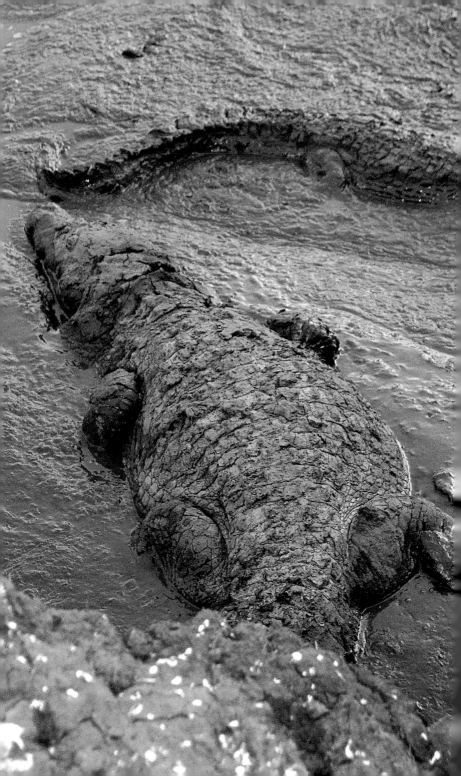

cles when opening. Which is why the so-called "crocodile wrestlers" sometimes seen on TV can hold a crocodile's jaws closed with their hands.

Crocodiles are interesting in other ways. They have more advanced hearts than other reptiles and their brains have a true cerebral cortex, making learned (as opposed to instinctive) behaviour possible, though this is refuted by at least one brain surgeon, who found that the crocodile's brain-case doesn't allow for much evolutionary expansion. But even if crocodiles are never going to pass a MENSA IQ test, a creature which has survived for 65 million years can't exactly be "dumb". And whatever they might lack in IQ, good looks and table manners, crocodiles can be caring. Females are very sensitive mothers, protecting their young for as long as two years.

Sexual maturity occurs at around 8 to 12 years. During mating, the male engages in elaborate displays to impress receptive females, copulation, which is brief, usually taking place on the river bed. After about two months the female scrapes a nesting site far enough from the water to avoid flooding, lays a few dozen chicken-sized eggs and covers them with organic debris. Ten weeks later the hatchlings (assuming the nest hasn't been discovered by various predators) emerge, calling for their mother. She collects them in her mouth and takes them down to the water.

Hippos, with their huge, balloon-like figures and indolent lifestyle, often figure, unlike the crocodile, as cuddly toys or cartoons. In reality they can be just as dangerous and must be treated with respect, ashore or afloat. Exclusively vegetarian, they tend to leave the water after dark to graze, though you will quite often see them grazing by day in Ruaha, wherever they feel safe. At night they might travel 10 km. or more, consuming large amounts of grass, though these represent less than 1.5% of their body weight, compared with 2.5% for most other ungulates. Presumably the hippo's laid-back lifestyle and the fact that its weight is often supported by water reduces the need to eat more. Certainly the hippo is in little danger of succumbing to anorexia.

Visitors often ask how long hippos can remain submerged. Experts disagree but it is safe to say that in natural circumstances, they rarely submerge for more than 3 – 5 minutes, increasing to 10 or more in extreme circumstances. What is more certain is

Left: Well-fed crocodile sleeps it off

that hippos, with few if any exceptions, mate and give birth in the water. Which, when you are as heavy as a pick-up truck and built like a balloon, seems to make sense.

Hippo Pool to Trekimboga

Having regained the main track upstream, you pass through a stretch of *Combretum* and soon come to another turn-off at R4, from which a short track brings you to a view point overlooking the Nyamakuyu Rapids. The rapids are not spectacular but this stretch of the river is attractive, dominated as it is by Chariwindi. Returning to R4 and driving south, you eventually cross several *korongos*, the Swahili name for a gully or watercourse (and also for "stork" or "roan antelope", so beware of confusions!).

You will sometimes see kudu, zebra, giraffe or sometimes bushbuck (*Tragelaphus scriptus*) drinking in the bed of such *korongos*, or feeding nearby. Along the intervening reaches of the river you might also see a herd of roan antelope. The Roan (*Hippotragus equinus*), sometimes also seen from the Lunda track or in the *Combretum*-covered hills close to Msembe, is slightly bigger than the Sable, which it rivals in magnificence, despite its shorter horns and less dramatic colour (a mixture of red-

dish fawn and grey). Its face is contrastingly marked in black and white. Said to be "very pugnacious and aggressive" by temperament, the roan is shy of humans and vehicles. The best time to see it is probably late morning, as they tend to drink between 9 am and midday.

On the subject of drinking, authorities in South Africa's Kruger National Park, to safeguard the park's estimated 1,000 roan, created lots of strategically placed water holes, only to see the roan population decline to forty-five! The authorities eventually realized that the extra water holes

attracted other game as well as roan, causing much greater competition for grazing, and thereby encouraging more lions to the area. The additional water holes have now been reduced by a third in an attempt to achieve the right balance. Interestingly enough, in the light of these findings, both roan and sable, in Ruaha, tend to occupy marginal areas, perhaps to avoid competition from other ungulates.

The adult roan has little need to avoid the Leopard (*Panthera pardus*), which like the bushbuck loves the well-screened security of the *korongos*. Leopards occur through-out the park and are regularly seen, though you still need luck to find one during a short visit. Like lions they seek the shade once the sun becomes too hot, which often means climbing into convenient trees, though they are frequently seen on or close to the ground, especially during cooler times of day.

Leopards have the widest distribution of all wild cats and survive in places where other animals would have been exterminated, sometimes living close to villages, their habitat ranging from near-desert to rain forest. Their diet is

Top: Hippo leaves the Ruaha to graze

similarly varied, including animals up to the size of impala and sometimes beyond (a leopard has been known to kill an adult eland, largest of the antelopes) and down to birds, dung beetles, frogs, crabs and even fish, pangolins and porcupines.

The leopard's habit of hauling prey high into trees is most often indulged where concentrations of lions or hyenas are high, such as the Serengeti. In Ruaha they are just as likely to eat their prey on the ground, though they might drag it into cover. They do, however, sometimes hoist their victim into surprisingly high branches, exhibiting great strength in the process. A leopard has been observed carrying the carcase of a young giraffe, two or three times its weight, almost 6 m. up into a tree, the equivalent of an average man lifting more than three times the basic airline baggage allowance over three times his own height.

Airline baggage aside, to see a leopard in the wild is one of the most exciting of safari experiences. The Cleopatra of the cat world combines a regal aloofness with an almost unparalleled beauty and a quiescent ferocity in the same seductive frame. The ferocity, when unleashed, is awesome, but leopards rarely attack humans without provocation. When left alone they are shy and retiring with regard to humans, and although the female leopard is "more deadly than the male", especially when guarding young cubs, she is, like the crocodile, a very attentive, devoted mother.

All this would hardly get a vote of confidence from the Bat-eared Fox (*Otocyon megalotis*) which is fair-

© Pietro Luraschi

ly often seen in Ruaha, among many other places in the open bush west of Ruaha River Lodge. For this much-loved creature could easily disappear down a leopard's gullet instead of its own burrow. A loop road, starting and ending on either side of the lodge and bisected by a more direct track from the lodge itself, provides access to this particular area.

The little silvery-buff foxes, with their bushy tails, huge ears and dark face-masks, might sometimes be seen outside their dens, despite being predominantly nocturnal. They usually live in pairs or small family groups, moving around at night to look for termites, beetles, eggs or nestlings of ground-nesting birds, lizards, fruits, bulbs and small rodents.

They will even eat scorpions and have been known to attack puff adders, one of the most dangerous of snakes.

Snakes are plentiful in Ruaha, from the highly venomous black mamba and puff adder to a host of harmless or near-harmless bush or sand snakes. The non-poisonous but huge African python is also found in the park, especially in areas close to water, where it will ambush rodents or small mammals, and sometimes larger animals, suffocating them by constriction (pythons don't crush their prey to death). Almost all snakes

Left: Giraffe making the most of the drying pools along the lower Mdonya
Top: Cleopatra of the cat world in reflective mood
Next page: Young vervet monkeys feeding

will get out of your way and even cobras and mambas are reluctant to strike unless provoked. Of course you need to be vigilant when walking around in the bush but the chances are that on a short safari you won't even see a snake. If you do, enjoy the experience, for snakes are always fascinating.

Plants can be poisonous, as well as snakes. The Fireball Lily (*Scadoxus multiflorus*) is one, though it isn't going to leap up and bite you, even if you tread on it. Which is unlikely, as the flower, which blossoms at the onset of the rains, is very conspicuous and beautiful. It is often found among rocky outcrops, such as those in this area, or in the shade of a tree or termite mound, where there is a high water table. As its popular name implies, the flower is a brilliant red spikeball, about 15 cm. in diameter, sometimes seen in clusters which startle you at first sight, amid the relative uniformity of the bush.

The "shaving brush" filaments of the fireball lily are also replicated, though in a straw-coloured crest, in a bird which is equally eye-catching, the Crowned Crane (*Balearica regulorum*), sometimes encountered, among other places, on the close-cropped swards of grassland that occur towards Trekimboga. One of the most elegant of a family known for its elegance, the crane's plumage is a delightful harmony of slate-grey, velvety black and snowy white, enriched by golden-saffron in the primaries and touches of bright red about the face, topped by the distinctive crown.

Trekimboga

Some 12/13 km or so upstream from the rocky outcrops on which the River Lodge is built is a spot known as Trekimboga. The name means "the cooking of the meat" in the language of the Hehe; no doubt Hehe hunters camped here in the past. If so they had good taste in more ways than one, for the area is quite scenic. An unmarked track leads from the main track to the river's edge, where you can park in the shade of an acacia. In the rainy season the Ruaha cascades between its banks in a series of rapids, affording fine views downstream, often enhanced, at all seasons, by impala, giraffe and zebra.

Impala are often ignored once they have been "ticked off", as they are so common, yet they are very unusual animals. Like all antelopes they are ruminants (they chew the cud). It might not look exciting but it is. The ruminant stomach has four chambers, the largest of which, the rumen, first receives the hastily chewed food. But the fascinating thing about rumination is that it involves countless microscopic creatures, some of which break down cellulose. More remarkably, the bacteria include "carnivores" as well as "herbivores", and live only for about 24 hours, their dead bodies providing an astonishing one-fifth of the ruminant's protein requirements.

The impala (*Aepyceros melampus*) is astonishing in itself; it is almost a living fossil. Throughout an evolutionary period when some of its nearest relatives have undergone almost twenty significant changes, the impala has remained much the same. Even nature, it seems, cannot improve on perfection. The impala, at least in form, is surely near-perfect, and imbued with an amazing grace. Beautiful to look at, with their elegant lines and the lyre-shaped horns of the male, impalas are also poetry in motion, wonderfully fluid jumpers capable of leaping 3 m. high and over 11 m. in length, the equivalent of jumping one-and-a-half cricket pitches whilst leaping over an elephant. Their collective leaping partly explains their evolutionary success, for it isn't merely haphazard but orientated towards other members of the group, one animal sometimes jumping over another, in a predator-confusing explosion of movement.

Characteristically you will see large harems of impala ewes under the watchful eye of a dominant ram. Rams have to fight for their privileges, though fights are usually ritualistic. Dominant males lose condition after a while, not because of their "super-stud" status, for copulation is brief, but because of the constant need to chase or challenge rivals, or shepherd the ewes into compliance, and the distraction from feeding which all this entails. There are, of course, always young challengers waiting, often in a nearby bachelor herd, to take over. But impala society is far from simplistic and bachelor groups will sometimes be allowed within dominant male's territory, to feed with impunity, as long as their body language is deferential.

Impala, like many other herbivores, are often hosts to one or other of the two ox-peckers found in Ruaha. It was once thought that herbivores welcomed the attentions of these birds, which help to rid their hosts of blood-sucking flies and ticks, but like most uninvited guests the birds seem to irritate rather than please. Which is probably why you don't see them on elephant, which could easily swipe the birds into oblivion with their trunks. Apart from their bills the two ash-brown oxpeckers are similar, though the Red-billed (*Buphagus erythrorhynchus*) has a yellow eye wattle. The Yellow-billed (*Buphagus africanus* - the bill is actually yellow with a red tip) is the more common in Ruaha.

Jongomero

Just over 20 km. west of Trekimboga, still following the river, you arrive by the confluence of the Ruaha and the Jongemero, and a ranger post. Here we leave the upstream drive as the Ruaha makes a fairly sharp turn south.

The track we have been following continues west, along the northern bank of the Jongomero, which feeds the Ruaha and which, for much of the year, is a sand river. The area around the confluence is known as Hussman's Bridge, after a gentleman who bridged a narrow stretch of the Ruaha here in the 1950s, to facilitate access to his timber logging business.

The bridge collapsed, taking the ill-fated Hussman with it, to his death, but the nearby hippo pool which Hussman would have known is still in use. In the dry season as many as 100 hippos and twice as many crocodiles might be seen here. The pool is a natural part of the river, half-enclosed by rock. To reach it you continue along the track, which heads uphill, and ignoring the turn off to Jongomero Camp (marked by a cairn about 3 km. from the ranger post) drive on for a further 6 or 7 km. until you come to the Jongomero River, or rather to its course, for the river would have to be dry to allow you to cross. Once on the far side you follow the signs to the pool, some 5 km. to the left.

Close to the point where the track crosses the bed of the Jongomero you will find yourself in the proximity of some attractive *Faidherbia albida* woodland, though this is accessible only via the track that leads to the ranger post at Magangwe, to the north-west, the superb old trees towering above you as you proceed before phasing into *Acacia sieberana* and *A. tortilis*.

Beautiful woodland is one of many appealing features of the Jongomero area, together with its "away-from-it-all" remoteness and the fine landscapes visible from various vantage points, and enhanced by the nearby Palangire Hills. Together, of course, with the always exciting river from which the locality takes its name, the Ruaha which it feeds and the many animal and bird species found throughout the area.

The Jongomero is bordered by typical riverine species, with *Combretum/Terminalia/Entandrophr agma* woodland away from the river, relieved in places by patches of relatively open grassland. One *Entandrophragma* found here, as elsewhere in Ruaha, is *E. caudatum*, known as the "Wooden Banana" due to its fruits, which resemble peeled bananas made of wood. Once the royal tree of Barotseland in Zambia, it was used to make royal barges for the Paramount Chief.

Some woodland in Jongomero is quite dense, which inevitably means tsetses, but which in turn

Left: Female impala - living fossils

means game. This includes huge herds of buffalo and smaller but impressive herds of eland. The eland (*Taurotragus oryx*) frequent various water holes during the dry season, which is interesting, as they can exist without drinking, obtaining moisture from succulents and other juicy plants. Yet when domesticated (the eland, one of the wildest and shyest of animals in the bush, takes astonishingly easily to domestication) eland drink as much as cattle. Once described as "the apotheosis of antelope evolution" the eland, despite being the largest of all antelopes, can clear obstacles 2 m. high and maintain a steady pace for many kilometres. To see a line of eland trotting heads high across the middle distance (they rarely let you get closer) is something old safari hands drool about, symbolic of "the real Africa" which they love but cannot always define.

The eland is more than 160 times heavier than Kirk's Dik-dik (*Madoqua kirkii*), another antelope found at Jongomero and throughout much of non-*Miombo* Ruaha. When alarmed the dik-dik, little bigger than a hare, makes a "zik-zik!" whistling noise through its flexible, elongated nose, which might explain its name. The nose also acts as a cooling device, much needed as small creatures overheat quickly. Rapid panting also helps the cooling process, and if this fails, dik-dik will lick their coats, reducing their temperature by evaporation. They live as monogamous pairs in a small territory which they know intimately, feeding mainly on the leaves of trees and shrubs, as well as choice grasses, herbs and sedges. Their high metabolic rate demands a low-fibre, easily digested diet.

The agility and awareness of these diminutive antelopes must be more than a match for the lumbering Honey Badger (*Mellivora capensis*) which despite the sweetness of its name would make short work of a dik-dik if it could. About the same size and shape as the European Badger, its "don't-even-think-about-it!" body language and warning colouration, black below and whitish-grey above, are enough to deter most enemies. Shy and fairly nocturnal, the badger can be fearlessly aggressive when provoked, capable, it is said, of killing game as large as buffalo, "biting the groin and genital organs, the animal then bleeding to death". Why a badger would wish to attach itself to a buffalo's groin remains unexplained, but it is obviously not a creature to trifle with.

Visitors needn't clad themselves in body armour. Like most wild creatures the badger will avoid confrontation unless molest-

ed, snuffling and shuffling around in search of food, which includes carrion and even scraps of food from the refuse dumps at camps and lodges. At certain seasons it tends to concentrate on bees' nests, and will climb trees to get at the honey and grubs.

It is sometimes led to these wild hives by the Greater Honey-guide (*Indicator indicator*), one of an abundance of interesting birds found around Jongomero. The honey-guide chatters and flashes its white outer tail feathers excitedly to indicate that a nest is nearby, making little looping flights until the nest site is reached, when it waits for the badger (or human being) to raid the nest. Later it will claim whatever dead bees, grubs or wax are left. All honey-guides

eat wax, the Indicator honey-guides from bee-hives, the others obtaining it from scale insects which they catch. Only the Scaly-throated seems to eat honey. And only *Indicator indicator* guides on a regular basis, though the Scaly-throated (*I. variegatus*) has been known to do so. Despite their fascinating relationship, honey-badger and honey-guide are able to find nests unassisted.

Other predators are found at Jongomero. In addition to the big cats they include wild dogs and spotted and striped hyenas. The Spotted Hyena (*Crocuta crocuta*), bolder and not quite so nocturnal as the Striped (*Hyaena hyaena*), and

Top: Dik-dik
Next page: Amazingly, the Honey Badger is capable of killing a buffalo such as this!

probably far more numerous, is seen fairly often, the Striped infrequently. Spotted hyenas form huge clans in Ngorongoro and the Serengeti but groupings are much smaller in Ruaha, though even individual hyenas are capable of killing a large variety of prey, as well as scavenging. Their sex lives are rather more complex, however, for Spotted Hyena society is dominated by the females, which outweigh males by about 6 kg. More confusingly, males and females, thanks to the elongated clitoris of the latter, have superficially similar genital organs, even when erect. It

doesn't confuse the hyenas; they just get on with it, but apparently in a very "civilized" manner. According to research the males have learned that aggression during or leading up to mating is counter-productive, and that "good manners" are rewarded. Or perhaps that when your mate is much bigger than you, discretion is the better part of ardour...

Mdonya Sand River

Jongomero is connected to another of Ruaha's interesting and relatively remote areas, Mdonya, by several good tracks, but we will

quite picturesque and good for lion and leopard it is worth a closer look before following the Mdonya upstream. Even in the dry season there are usually several pools in the river bed here, surrounded by clusters of rocks and clumps of trees and palms and bush, all of which, with Kimilimitonge in the background, makes a pleasing – and in terms of game viewing promising - scene.

Lesser kudu are sometimes seen in the nearby *Combretum* and rock hyraxes on the boulders by the drift (a causeway across the Mdonya). A small network of tracks, on either side of the drift, allows you to explore the immediate vicinity north and south of the river, much covered by professional driver/guides, who know a good "big cat" area when they see one. Big cats or not, it is always worth a detour, for giraffe, zebra, buffalo and impala often come to drink here, and elephants sometimes pass through.

The giraffe (*Giraffa camelopardalis*), like the elephant, needs no introduction. There are 8 recognized races, but only one in Tanzania, the Maasai or Common Giraffe (*G.c.tippelskirchii*). It can attain a height of 5.5 m. from hooves to horns and is the world's largest ruminant. Numerous throughout

begin this particular "drive" from a more central location, the crossroads (marker cairn R 7) a little way up the slope from the bridge at Ibuguziwa. Heading from here to the Mdonya Drift you have to be alert, for you need to turn left before crossing the drift, at marker D 11, and the present sign says "Nyakatowo" rather than Mdonya. Nyakatowo, in fact, is a tributary of the Mdonya. For most of the year both are sand rivers.

The Mdonya Drift (between D 11 and D 12) lies at the south-eastern corner of Kimilimitonge, and as the area adjacent to the drift is

below-the-escarpment Ruaha, the giraffe browses on a wide variety of trees and shrubs but feeds by choice on *Acacia* or *Combretum*. The observant visitor will often recognize "giraffe country", for the animals prune many trees into distinctive shapes through constant browsing, plucking leaves, sometimes from wickedly armed thorn trees, with their 45 cm. tongues, as expertly as tea-pickers.

Returning to the track which leads to Mdonya Falls, we head west along the Mdonya's southern bank, by-passing two public camp sites, by the river. The track crosses the southern sector of the Gomhungire Mbuga, *mbuga* being Swahili for seasonally swampy black-cotton grassland, between the Mdonya and the Nyakatowo. Black cotton soil (cotton is grown on it in the Sudan) is a nightmare for drivers when it turns to mud; a vehicle can slide into a trough up to its axles and be stuck for hours. In the dry season it cracks and hardens into bone-shaking bumps and hollows. All in all, black cotton soil is not very driver-friendly, but on this particular track you needn't be too concerned, as it has been overlaid with murram.

Towards the escarpment you enter a swathe of riverine woodland, characterized by wonderful old figs (*Ficus spp.*), *Faidherbia albida*, *Acacia tortilis*, *A. sieberana*, *Lonchocarpus capassa* and *Diospyros mespiliformis*. The *Lonchocarpus* is one of several unrelated trees which attract small insects known as frog-hoppers, the nymphs of which suck sap voraciously from the tree and with almost similar speed eject near-pure water. This phenomenon can produce pools of water under the tree for a week or more in the dry season, giving rise to much superstition among many rural Tanzanians, who know the trees as "rain trees". This lovely belt of woodland, interspersed with little glades where you are always likely to see elephant, giraffe, impala and other game, extends to the Falls and the nearby Mdonya Old River Camp.

The Falls themselves, when in full flow, cascade down the broken, rocky slope of the escarpment into the boulder-strewn bed below, hidden among a tangled grove of trees and shrubs. As waterfalls go they are fairly ordinary, but their location on the edge of the escarpment and the tangle of vegetation at their foot gives them additional appeal, for a variety of birds might be seen here, including, if you are lucky, the colourful Violet-crested Turaco (*Tauraco porphyreolophus*), with its iridescent violet head and crest, grey legs and belly, violet and blue tail and wings of azure and crimson. The crimson-red flight feathers, so

striking in flight, owe their colour to pigment, not refraction of the light as in many birds, which is why they are conspicuous even in the gloom of the gallery forest.

Within easy driving distance of Mdonya Camp are three springs close to the foot of the Makinde escarpment. To the south-west are Makinde and Mkwawa, not too far apart and worth the drive, though it is advisable to set off early before the tsetses become too active. Freshwater springs, especially in the dry season, are usually well-frequented by game. Lichtenstein's Hartebeeste (*Sigmoceros lichtensteinii*) characteristically a *Miombo* species, is sometimes seen by Makinde. Previously considered a subspecies of the common hartebeest it has recently been upgraded to a species in its own right.

North-east of the Mdonya Falls are the Mwayembe Springs. It is possible to make a pleasant morning's round trip from Mdonya Camp, along the foot of the escarpment to the springs, returning southwards across the open, baobab-studded grasslands of the Gomhungire Mbuga, bringing you back to the main Mdonya track. The springs are backed by a screen of woodland that lies

Top: The world's largest ruminant browsing on acacia leaves
Next page: The "Real Africa" - sunlit expanses of the Ruaha Valley by Msembe

between them and the escarpment, but the country to the south is relatively open, reducing, to some extent, the number of tsetses.

Above this pleasing scene the 1828 m. high Ndanyanwa rises from the plateau above the escarpment. It is said to be haunted by herds of phantom cattle, though the origin of this myth is lost in time. A variety of wilder, more substantial animals, including giraffe, zebra, impala, warthog and yellow baboons visits the springs themselves, but a cautious approach is necessary as the game here is still unused to sudden disturbances. Lions find Mwayembe and the other springs rewarding at times, and the area along the escarpment wall, with its rocky shelves and crevices, thick tree cover of trees and access to per-manent fresh water, is ideal for leopard.

The wide-ranging and endangered wild dog (*Lycaon pictus*) sometimes turns up at Mwayembe, as elsewhere. A group of 46 has been seen in recent years, though between 6 - 16 is the norm. Much maligned in the past, these "painted wolves" (they are not true dogs), often beautifully marked in patches and whorls of black and tan and white, are now better understood, despite their habit of pursuing victims relentlessly before ripping them apart and often eating them alive. They are, after all, doing what they have evolved to do in the most efficient way, and cruelty, like compassion, is a human attribute (except, perhaps, for chimpanzees).

In fact wild dogs are extremely

© Pietro Luraschi

sociable and "caring", among themselves. Healthy animals have been seen feeding, by regurgitation, injured or disabled packmates, and however distressing their method of killing to human sensitivities there is no "savage" or "selfish" in-fighting over the meat, as with lions. Even pups are raised communally, with male dogs taking much of the responsibility. Interestingly, only the so-called "alpha" male and female dogs mate, actively preventing other dogs from doing so, though the alpha male will sometimes mate with a subordinate female. Aggression within the pack is rare, though females denied the right to breed occasionally (and understandably!) fight for the privilege. Life can't be too much fun for sub-ordinate males, either, which often outnumber females.

Another myth concerning wild dogs is that they chase prey in relays, the leading dog replaced, when tiring, by a fresher one. In fact this happens coincidentally, when the prey changes direction and another dog tries to intercept. Otherwise the alpha male normally leads until it comes up with the prey, when it attempts to hold or distract it until other dogs arrive. Hunting normally takes place in the mornings and early evenings, or on moonlit nights, with medium-sized animals such as impala preferred, though smaller or larger animals might be singled out.

Left: Wild dogs contest remnants of kill, but not aggressively
Top: Resting after the morning hunt

Wild dogs might be encountered almost anywhere in the park, but that other diurnal predator the cheetah (*Acinonyx jubatus*), which relies on speed rather than stamina, prefers more open areas, such as the grassy mbuga south of Mwayembe. Nothing is certain in the bush, however, and cheetahs might easily be seen in *Combretum/Commiphora* woodland or other "unlikely" habitats. Among their favourite prey species is the Grant's Gazelle, found almost exclusively in open grassland, particularly north and south of the Mwagusi.

The cheetah's speed has often been exaggerated. It is certainly impressive – a cheetah can achieve 75 kmph. in under 3 seconds from a standing start, with a top speed of about 100 kmph. Like all cats, however, the cheetah rarely does more than is necessary, and will often hold its top speed in reserve. The body temperature of a cheetah racing flat out rises alarmingly quickly, to a point where brain damage would result if the pace was maintained. Which helps to explain why approximately half their hunts end in failure.

If you are staying overnight at Mdonya Old River Camp (or any other) you might see a rather smaller, mainly nocturnal spotted predator, the genet. Frequently regarded as a cat it actually belongs

in the *Viverridae* family with civets and mongooses, though it does have a somewhat cat-like face and retractile claws. Both the Larger Spotted Genet (*Genetta tigrina*) and the Smaller Spotted (*Genetta genetta*) occur in Ruaha, often in or around one of the camps, as they quickly adapt to an easy life eating scraps of meat put out by the kitchen staff. Their natural diet consists of small mammals (especially rodents), frogs, termites, millipedes, scorpions, birds, eggs and so on, though they also eat certain fruits. At ease in trees as well as on the ground, unlike other members

of their family, the slender, long-tailed genets move through the branches with a sinuous grace.

Above the Escarpment

Until recently most of above-the-escarpment Ruaha was inaccessible to tourists, and much of it still is. But a new track which links with an older one now allows more adventurous travellers (and those who can live with tsetse flies) to drive between Mwagusi and Mdonya camps (or of course vice-versa) by ascending the escarpment at one end and descending at the other, providing

some experience of *Miombo* country and its attractions. You won't see great congregations of animals or birds but those species you do see might be pretty exciting, as *Miombo* is a fairly specialized habitat.

Assuming you begin at Mwagusi you take the Mpululu track (Mpululu being the site of a ranger post on the Mzombe River) and soon begin the escarpment ascent. You will be rewarded, if you stop and look back, with fine

Top: Top athletes taking a breather – two cheetahs resting

views. The track then passes through a belt of mixed *Combretum*, where sable can often be seen, before leading through an area known as Ikuka Flats, an old lake bed crossed by an ancient elephant trail which is still in use. Among other species of game giraffe, zebra, and lion might be encountered here.

Some 49 km. or so from Mwagusi Camp you turn left, and pass through open *Miombo*. About 18 km. beyond this left turn you will see a turn-off to the right, which would, if you took it, eventually bring you within 2 km. of the Mzombe River. Ignoring this turn-off, however, you continue to the south-west. Throughout this particular section there are places which afford lovely views over the park towards the distant Ruaha. Elephants are sometimes found here also.

You next cross an *mbuga*, where great numbers of waxbills and cordon bleus sometimes congregate and where, if you are lucky, you might come across oribi. The Oribi (*Ourebia ourebi*) is a small but elegant antelope, sometimes mistaken for the common duiker. The oribi, however, has a more slender build and a longer neck, with a distinctive gland, in the form of a circular black patch, below the relatively large ear.

At one point you negotiate a steep gully which is, in fact, the source of the Mwagusi River. Beyond the gully you find yourself among a pleasant area of open *Combretum* which again allows expansive views across the Ruaha Valley. The more immediate surroundings can be attractive also; in July or August, when the woodland leaves are yellowing and the skies often blue you might find yourself in a van Gogh painting that never was, with the same uncompromising colours but with *Combretum* in place of cornfields.

The track bends around Ndanyana Hill before winding slowly down to the escarpment wall again by Mwayembe Springs, from where you can complete the circuit back to Mwagusi or go to Mdonya. The complete circuit would be a longish drive in the bush (around 150 km.) so notify your camp or the park authorities of your intentions if travelling independently, leave lots of time and take adequate food and drink. Of course you could always drive part way, from either end, and turn back whenever you wish. Whatever the case, it is an area of much potential.

Left: Sinuosly graceful genet
Next page: Martial Eagle feeds on impala lamb which it probably killed

POSTSCRIPT
RUAHA'S BIRDS

More and more visitors to the parks are interested in birds, and more and more camps and lodges are offering guided "bird walks", led by experts, as an optional extra. Ruaha, with its current list of 526 species, is a delight for birders, serious or otherwise. In a booklet such a this it is impossible to highlight more than a few token species, but the following paragraphs, kindly donated by a keen birder, might serve as an "aperitif". A comprehensive bird list is usually on sale at the park gate or in the camps and lodges.

The birdlife of Ruaha is, for the most part, less dependent on the river than most large mammals but some of the bigger avian attractions are riverine species, the most conspicuous being the White-headed Plover. Every stretch of shingle bank seems to have a noisy and excitable resident pair. African skimmers also nest in these exposed places but are harder to find. The best time to look for them is when they are feeding at dusk and dawn.

Over much of Africa giant kingfishers are found on large rivers with well-developed vegetation along the banks; in Ruaha they are common and sometimes remarkably "tame" and there cannot be many places where this spectacular bird is easier to see. They are well-named and are actually slightly larger than the green-backed herons that frequent the same habitat.

With patience and luck the rare White-backed Night Heron can be found at its daytime roost. With even greater good fortune Pel's Fishing Owl could turn up; the best chance is if one of these magnificent birds is disturbed during the day. A much smaller member of the owl family, the Pearl-spotted Owlet, is often seen during the day.

The Violet-tipped Courser, a nocturnal member of the wader group, is common but only likely to be encountered on the roads at night or, like Temminck's Courser, on recently-burned areas.

Crowned cranes are most likely to be seen in the wet season when they are vocal and the strange trumpeting calls and various cat-like and querulous sounds can be heard.

Verreaux's Eagle is not an easy bird to see in Tanzania but can be seen on Kimilimitonge or on the

© Pietro Luraschi

rocky outcrops close to the River Lodge. In the vicinity of *Hyphaene ventricosa* palms it is worth searching for red-necked falcons. Driving in and out of the park, especially along the "Never Ending Road", can produce a party of the rather comical crested guineafowl in the thick scrubby woodland outside the boundary. Another elusive gamebird, Shelley's Francolin, occurs on dry open hillsides.

What was considered to be a race of Bennett's Woodpecker is now considered to be a full species – the Speckle-throated Woodpecker. In East Africa the range of this bird is only south-western Tanzania so it is worth searching for.

The Uhehe Fiscal, which looks rather like a Pied Wagtail, has an even smaller range and is another bird sometimes separated from a commoner relative. Ruaha is a good place to find great spotted cuckoos; there seem to be both resident birds and migrants from Europe.

Left: Hooded Vulture - note the slender hooked bill which enables the species to pierce the tough hides of large dead animals
Top: The Ruaha Red-billed Hornbill – now known to be a separate species
Next page: If you've got it, flaunt it – Crowned Crane presents his credentials

ACCOMMODATION GUIDE

Mwagusi Sand River Camp

Small, exclusive tented camp owned and personally supervised by Chris Fox, one of a family of long-time Tanzanian residents with great experience of the bush and of Ruaha. Situated alongside the Mwagusi, overlooking a sector of the sand river, just north of Mwagusi Causeway. Attractive location, good international cuisine, dinner often taken under the stars. Well-designed thatched and half-walled dining room, lounge etc built from local materials. Ten luxury tents, enclosed in thatched, open-sided bandas (huts) to blend with the natural surroundings, including two "honeymoon suites". Game drives, walking safaris, fly-camping are normally available as optional extras.

www.ruaha.org

Jongomero Tented Camp

Beautifully designed luxury safari camp imaginatively set among riverine woodland at the edge of the Jongomero Sand River, which feeds the nearby Ruaha, in the remote and attractive south-

---

Left: Blending in - a thatched banda at Mwagusi Sand Rivers Camp

western sector of the park. Accommodation comprises eight large, well-appointed tents under huge thatched roofs, each tent with a spacious and private verandah (privacy being an essential part of Jongomero's charm). Very original dining and living areas, excellent international cuisine. A pool allows visitors to cool off in the heat of the day – more active pursuits in the cooler mornings and evenings include game drives with qualified, experienced guides. www.selous.com

Ruaha River Lodge
Longest established camp in Ruaha and enduringly popular. Prime location among and around rocky outcrops alongside the Ruaha River, upstream of the park entrance bridge and across from Chariwindi Mountain. Owned and run by members of the Fox family, (long-time Tanzanian residents who know Ruaha well). Recently reorganised to embrace two separate camps, each self-contained to provide privacy without losing the congenial atmosphere for which the River Lodge has long been known. Twenty-five unpretentious but comfortable bandas (huts) of local stone and thatch (presently being upgraded), good homely food, much of the produce flown in from the Fox family farm in the neighbouring highlands. Game drives, walking safaris, fly-camping are normally available as optional extras. www.tanzaniasafaris.info

Mdonya Old River Camp
Small, simple tented camp under the escarpment alongside old Mdonya River bed, now a sand

river, close to the present Mdonya River and the Mdonya Falls. Situated among beautiful riverine woodland. Mdonya has an easy-going, warm atmosphere, reflecting the personality of its owner and manager. Simple, international cuisine with an Italian influence. Eight comfortable tents, with shower and toilet facilities enclosed by canvas but otherwise open to the stars. Game drives to various springs around the camp, full day game drive along the Ruaha River, early morning birding walks around the camp or walking safaris along the sand river.

www.adventurecamps.co.tz

Tandala Camp

Set among lovely Acacia tortilis woodland close to the Iringa-Ruaha track, a little way from the park entrance, and named after the Lesser Kudu which, with other game, is found in the area. Eleven luxury tents on stilted platforms, swimming pool, pleasant, welcoming ambience, excellent international cuisine with Mediterranean influence (one of the co-owners is Greek). Owners farm land adjacent to the Iringa-Ruaha track so much of the produce is home-grown. Game drives into the park available now (April 2004), local foot safaris and birding walks a possibility in the future. Birding around the camp already good.

tandala@bushlink.co.tz
tandalaruaha@hotmail.com

Self-catering Bandas/Camping within the Park

Self-catering Bandas

These uniport huts and simple dining room are situated by the Ruaha close to the park headquarters at Msembe. Bedding, cooking

Left: Jongomeru Tented camp
Bottom left: Ruaha River Lodge
Bottom right: Mdonya Old River Camp

utensils etc provided. Basic facilities but a pleasant location. Advanced booking, through the Tourism Officer, Ruaha NP, PO Box 369, Iringa.

Camping

There are public and "special" (private) campsites in the park, the two public ones being alongside the Mdonya River close to marker D 11. Write to the Tourism Officer, Ruaha NP, PO Box 369 or see the ranger at the park gate. Don't expect too much in the way of facilities.

Accommodation in Iringa/Mufindi Area

There are various small hotels and guest houses in Iringa itself, and several farms, lodges or campsites in the Iringa/Ruaha area all offering good accommodation at reasonable or low budget prices. Most of them are too far from the park for day visits but they represent convenient stop-overs en route or as relaxing respites from safari routine. Only two are mentioned below but there are others. Ask around for up - to - date information.

Foxes Highland Lodge

Mufindi tea-growing area of Southern Highlands. Farm-based lodge owned and operated by long-term Tanzanian residents of English descent, who also own the River Lodge in Ruaha. Very homely, restful atmosphere, pleasant highland scenery, good food and company, cool mountain air, walking, riding, biking, fishing etc. **www.tanzaniasafaris.info**

Kisolanza Farm

Another lovely, homely farm-based retreat, 36 km or so west of Iringa, off the main Iringa-Mbeya road. Owned and run for more than 70 years by another fascinating family of one-time expatriates who made Tanzania their home, set in attractive gardens among typical Southern Highland country. Self-catering and camping as well as regular board.
www.kisolanza.com

Campsites Outside the Park

The following information has been kindly provided by Mr Richard Phillips, who knows the Ruaha area well:

Tungamalenga Campsite

Located in Tungamalenga village on the "villages road" to the park. Small but nice campsite with bar, restaurant and rooms. Close to the road, which can be a disadvantage due to passing traffic, but otherwise a handy and pleasant place to stay. Simple rooms available as well as camping area.

Left: Knob-billed Duck goes through his exercise routine
Top: Two cow buffalo close to one of the camps
Next Page: Lions are forced to prey heavily on buffalo in Ruaha - here a young male feeds on buffalo carcase

PARK MANAGEMENT AND CONSERVATION

I n a book such as this, intended for the caring, well-informed but non-specialist visitor with limited time, the topic of park management and conservation can only be discussed briefly. This is not to minimize the importance of the subject, only to acknowledge its complexities.

One of the greatest changes in park management and conservation policies over the years is the gradual evolution from solutions imposed arbitrarily from outside, with little if any consultation with local people, to the modern belief that the co-operation of such people is vital to successful management and conservation.

All Tanzanian parks now have some form of "outreach" programme, in which various dedicated organizations and individuals, from within the parks and from outside, work with local villages towards a better understanding of the authorities' – and the villagers' - problems and objectives, in an interactive and hopefully sensitive way.

Ruaha is more fortunate than many in having a very well-informed and energetic supporting body, the Friends of Ruaha Society (FORS), as

Left: Beautifully marked wild dogs - much in need of conservation

spearhead of the park's outreach activities. FORS, in close consultation with park authorities, works in areas adjacent to the park, mainly in the Idodi Division but also in Pawaga, currently (Feb 2005) reaching out to 10 out of the 19 villages in the region. The project includes environmental education in primary schools and clubs in secondary schools, various micro-enterprise programmes and a scholarship programme for Pasiansi Wildlife College. Other developments are under discussion.

Also involved is the MBOMI-PA Association (the acronym in translation stands for "Sustainable Use of Wildlife Resources in Idodi and Pawaga"), the local compo-nent of the old British Department for International Development (DFID). It has been in operation for five years, engaged in piloting implementation of Tanzania's new Wildlife Policy with particular emphasis on community-run Wildlife Management Areas (WMAs). The Association has worked closely with the National Parks during development of the policy and guidelines at national level, and is much in demand by people from all over Tanzania wanting to bene-fit from its experience.

Although the original project which MBOMIPA took over came to an end in 2001, the association was reborn the following year and numbers all 19 villages in Idodi

and Pawaga among its members. Each village provides two elected representatives to the MBOMIPA council which itself has an internally elected body. It also has a Board of Trustees, including the Friends of Ruaha Society and Ruaha's Chief Park Warden.

MBOMIPA is the first association of its kind (following the new Wildlife Management Area guidelines), its stated purpose to manage key natural resources in what will hopefully become one of Tanzania's first gazetted WMA, intended to ensure sustainable use of the resources under its control. As a new (or born-again) organization with much inertia and many difficulties to overcome it needs all the support it can get, and is eager

to ally itself with private or voluntary sector partners in and beyond Tanzania. The Friends of Ruaha Society already supports MBOMIPA wherever it can.

The park itself, with advice when required from various outside organisations, and under the umbrella of the Tanzanian National Parks Authority (TANAPA) also has its own (and national) management plans covering the short and longer term and embracing specific as well as general issues.

Left: Plants, such as this baobab, need to be protected
Top: Without co-operation from people outside the park, the Ruaha River as well as the animals that depend upon it is doomed
Page 144: Fine Greater Kudu Male

Bibliography

Antelopes (C.A. Spinage) – Croom Helm

Birds of Kenya and Northern Tanzania (D Zimmerman, D Turner and D Pearson) – Helm, London

East Africa (Jan Knappert) - Sangam Books

Field Guide to Birds of East Africa (T Stevenson and J Fanshawe) – Poyser, London

Field Guide to the Larger Mammals of East Africa (Dorst & Dandelot) – Collins

Maasai Women (Ulrike von Mitzlaff) - Trickster Tanzania Publishing House

Mammals of Africa (Haltenorth & Diller) – Collins

Miombo Magazine (various editions) – WCST

National Parks of East Africa (John G Williams) – Collins

Ruaha National Park – a guide (Anon) - Tanzanian National Parks

Ruaha National Park Bird List (Robert Glen) – Robert Glen

Ruaha National Park brochure (Friends of Ruaha Society/Sue Stolberger) – Friends of Ruaha Soc.

Ruaha Sketch Book (Sue Stolberger) – Sue Stolberger

Tanzania- African Eden (Javed Jafferji/Graham Mercer) – Gallery Publications

The Behaviour Guide to Africa's Mammals (Richard Estes) – Russel Friedman

The Bee-Eaters (CH Fry) – T & AD Poyser

The Kingdon Field Guide to African Mammals (Jonathan Kingdon) – A & CB

Tanganyika Notes & Records (various editions) – Tanganyika Society

Trees of Southern Africa (Keith Coates Palgrave) – Struik

Wild Flowers of East Africa (Michael Blundell) – Collins

Wild Lives (Doreen Wolfsen McColaugh) – African Wildlife Foundation

Useful Addresses

Postal

Tanzania National Parks, PO Box 3134 Arusha, Tanzania

Ruaha National Park, PO Box 369, Iringa, Tanzania

Friends of Ruaha, PO Box 7589, Dar es Salaam, Tanzania

Rob Glen, Ruaha National Park, PO Box 369, Iringa, Tanzania (for anyone with additions & interesting observations regarding the Ruaha bird list)

Useful Website Addresses and Websites Visited (Internet)

Tanzanian National Parks - www.habari.co.tz/tanapa/

Tanzania Tourist Board - www.tanzaniatouristboard.com

Friends of Ruaha - www.friendsofruaha.org/

Wildlife, trees etc: www.seaworld.org/AnimalBytes

www.sailfish.exis.net

www.kenyabeasts.org

www.press.jhu.edu/books/walkers_mammals_of_the_world/.html

www.plantapalm.com

www.york.ac.uk/res/celp/webpages/projects/ecology/tree%20guide/guide.htm

www.wildwatch.com

www.bbc.co.uk/nature/wildfacts

www.awf.org/wildlives

www.tanzaniabirdatlas.com (Neil and Liz Baker)

www.ecotravel.co.za/Guides/Wildlife

www.safaricamlive.com/Encyclopedia/mammals/duiker/Common%20Duiker%20I
nfo.htm

www.elephant.elehost.com

www.sandiegozoo.org

www.kidcyber.com

www.zoo.org

www.lynx.uio.no/catfolk/afrleo02.htm

The Internet's World Wide Web (www) is a treasure trove of interesting facts and figures about Ruaha, its camps and lodges, the travel and safari companies who operate
there, its wildlife, plants etc etc. The addresses I have visited have been too numerous to
mention or acknowledge here, other than the sample shown above, but anyone familiar
with the Net can type one or two key words into a search engine (I used "Google") and
come up with a plethora of websites. Some sites, like some books, are better than others, but you will discover the better ones for yourself. Those unfamiliar with the Net
should not be deterred – it is a simple matter (assuming you have access to a computer
and the Net itself!) and with the help of a friend, assistant at your local library etc you
will soon become proficient.

OTHER BOOKS PUBLISHED BY
GALLERY PUBLICATIONS

A Taste of Zanzibar - Zarina Jafferji & Javed Jafferji
A mouth-watering selection of Zanzibar's finest recipes to set your taste buds tingling with memories of your stay in Zanzibar.

Dhow Chasing in Zanzibar Waters - Captain G L Sullivan
An action-packed autobiographical account of the efforts of British naval Captain to help suppress the illegal sea trade in slaves in the Indian Ocean.

Doors of Zanzibar - Mwalim A Mwalim
Celebrates the intricate detail and beauty of Zanzibar's carved wooden doors, exploring Indian, Arabic and Swahili influences. Illustrated with stunning photographs.

Historical Zanzibar - Romance of the Ages
Professor Abdul Sheriff & Javed Jafferji
Illustrated account of Zanzibar's turbulent past, with archive photographs of the slave and ivory trade, life in the palace, the Shortest War in History and colonial rule.

Images of Lamu - Elie Losleben & Javed Jafferji
Images of Lamu is a photographic book of the culture, history and architecture of Kenya's northern archipelago. A UNESCO World Heritage Site, Lamu has captivated travelers for generations.

Images of Zanzibar - Bethan Rees Jones & Javed Jafferji
Glossy coffee-table book packed with stunning photographs from across Zanzibar and Pemba, including Stone Town, landscapes, beaches, culture, and aerial shots.

Life of Frederick Courtney Selous - J.G Millais
Autobiography of the famous hunter, explorer, naturalist, patriot and pioneer, providing a glimpse into the life of an extraordinary Englishman in the heyday of colonial Africa.

Lake Manyara National Park - Graham Mercer & Javed Jafferji
A park often overlooked by passing visitors.This book should put Manyara back where it belongs, among the very best of Tanzania's wonderful sanctuaries. Excellent Photographs.

Memoirs of an Arabian Princess from Zanzibar
Emily Reute
Written by Princess Salme, who eloped with a German trader, this autobiography provides an absorbing account of life in the harem and the palaces during the sultanate rule.
Also available in French, Italian, Spanish and German

Magic of Zanzibar - Gemma Pitcher & Javed Jafferji
A handy pocket-sized book of photographs for visitors to take home. Zanzibar's architecture, natural history, culture and colourful people are all depicted in full colour.

Mikumi National Park - Graham Mercer & Javed Jafferji
For too long Mikumi has been one of East Africa's most underrated parks. This book should change all that. It includes a fascinating history of the area as well as many insights into the park itself. Superb photographs.

Ngorongoro Conservation Area. - Graham Mercer & Javed Jafferji
What more can be written about this jewel in Tanzania's tourist-attraction crown? Quite a lot, as this book shows. Much of the information will be new to many people, and the whole Conservation Area is covered, not just the famous Crater. Top class photographs to match.

Serengeti National Park - Graham Mercer & Javed Jafferji
The Serengeti, with its astonishing seasonal migration, is the world's most famous national park, yet this new guide book treats it in a refreshingly individual and interesting way, made even more interesting by up-to-date information on the park and its wonderful wildlife. Illustrated by excellent photographs.

Selous Game Reserve - Rolf Baldus, Ludwig Siege & Javed Jafferji
The Selous is the largest protected area in Africa and home of most spectacular wildlife. This travel guide contains everything the visitor needs to know: wildlife, landscape, history; access by road, air and rail; up to date information on lodges, camping, walking safaris; park fees and many more valuable tips. It is the only reliable source of information on this unknown destination.

Safari Elegance - Amanda Harley & Javed Jafferji

Capturing the spirit of romance and adventure in the heart of the African wilderness, Safari Elegance celebrates the best of Kenya's safari design against the dramatic backdrop of the country's diverse landscape. Created as havens of elegance and style, the exclusive tented camps and lodges blend effortlessly with the natural beauty of an ancient land steeped in history and woven with legends.

Safari Kitchen - Amanda Harley & Javed Jafferji

A glossy coffee table style cookbook featuring the very best of Kenya's safari cuisine - from breakfast in the bush, to sundowners and sumptuous dinners served in elegant surroundings. Fabulous still-life shots of prepared dishes are combined with images of unique dining experiences in the heart of the wilderness, and interior design shots of the lodges and camps.

Safari Living - Gemma Pitcher & Javed Jafferji

Glossy coffee table book exploring the neglected area of Tanzania's design heritage, celebrating the style of the country's luxury safari lodges and private homes.

Safari Living Recipes - Gemma Pitcher and Javed Jafferji

Accompanying 'designer' cookbook featuring handpicked recipes from Tanzania's top safari lodges and camps.

Simply Zanzibar - Gemma Pitcher & Javed Jafferji

A lush, full colour coffee table book celebrating the unique visual appeal of the Spice Islands Zanzibar and Pemba. Hundreds of full colour photographs accompanied by informative text.

Sowing the Wind, Pemba before the Revolution Maulid M Haji

Autobiographical novel exploring life and politics through the eyes of its central character, Maulid, in the turbulent years leading up to independence, an d the subsequent revolution in 1964.

Swahili Style - Elie Losleben & Javed Jafferji

Swahili Style covers the design and architecture of the Swahili Coast of Kenya and Tanzania, featuring exclusive properties and private homes that have taken their inspiration from the old stone towns and coral palaces of the Indian Ocean coastline.

Swahili Kitchen - Elie Losleben & Javed Jafferji
Swahili Kitchen features the best of Swahili cooking as served in the area's best lodges. From the beaches of Kenya and Tanzania, full menus using island spices and fresh Indian Ocean catch are a perfect way to remember East Africa.

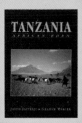

Tanzania African Eden - Graham Mercer & Javed Jafferji
Beautifully illustrated and well-written tribute to Tanzania's many attractions, in coffee table format – a wonderful gift for anyone living in Tanzania, visiting it or for armchair travelers who want to experience this astonishing part of East Africa at second-hand.

The Krazy Kanga Book - Pascal Bogaert
A distinctly off-beat book looking at some of the more bizarre aspects of East Africa's favourite garment - the kanga. Illustrated with lively and entertaining sketches showing the endless uses for kanga and how to wear them.

Tippu Tip, His Career in Zanzibar and Central Africa - Dr Heinrich Brode
New edition of Dr Brode's highly readable account of the life and times of Zanzibar's most notorious slave trader, his relationships with explorers Livingstone, Cameron, Stanley and Wissman, and his role in the international expedition to rescue Emin Pasha.

Tarangire National Park - Graham Mercer & Javed Jafferji
For years Tarangire was almost unknown except to a select group of "old Africa hands", who were happy to have the place to themselves. That has now changed, and an increasing number of tourists are discovering the park each year. This book, written by someone who first visited Tarangire in 1977, should help to explain why. As should the fine photographs by the celebrated Zanzibari photographer Javed Jafferji.

Zanzibar, A Plan for the Historic Stone Town Francesco Siravo & Stefano Bianca
Packed with historical information, plans photographs and illustrations, this reference book takes a detailed look at Zanzibar's history and architecture, and the future preservation of Stone Town.

Zanzibar in Contemporary Times - Robert Nunez Lyne
Focuses on the nineteenth century, detailing the consolidation of Omani Arab power from the Gulf to Zanzibar, the arrival of the British, and the struggle against the slave trade.

Zanzibar Stone Town, An Architectural Exploration Professor Abdul Sheriff & Javed Jafferji
A pocket-sized guide examining the unique blend of architectural styles that make up Zanzibar's historic quarter, illustrated with sketches and colour photographs.

Zanzibar Style - Gemma Pitcher & Javed Jafferji
A sumptuous full colour coffee table book celebrating the natural style of the island's inhabitants, exploring themes inspiring Zanzibar's architecture and interior design.
Available in Spanish, French, Italian and German

Zanzibar Style Recipes - Gemma Pitcher & Javed Jafferji
Accompanying 'designer' cookbook featuring a selection of dishes from Zanzibar's upmarket hotels and resorts.

Zanzibar Tales - George Bateman
A lively and entertaining translation of Swahili folktales passed down from generation to generation.

Zanzibar - An Essential Guide - Amanda Harley & Javed Jafferji
All the essential information for visitors seeking to discover this tropical paradise. Lush spice plantations, historic ruins, the narrow streets of Stone Town and pristine beaches lapped by the turquoise waters of the Indian Ocean are but a few of the gems waiting to be discovered. Fringed by colourful coral reefs, Zanzibar also offers an underwater Eden for divers and snorkellers.

All books distributed by:
Zanzibar Gallery, Mercury House, P O Box 3181, Zanzibar,
e mail: gallery@swahilicoast.com

INDEX

About the Author

Graham Mercer experienced his first East African safari as a young sailor with the British Royal Navy in 1962, in Kenya, and first went to Ruaha in 1978. He has visited the park many times throughout the intervening years. Since 1977 he has been based at the International School of Tanganyika in Dar es Salaam, and has visited all the Tanzanian national parks, some of them often.

The BBC Wildlife Magazine, after he won its prestigious essay-writing prize in 1988, referred to him as one of "Britain's best nature writers". Since then he has had eight books published, all on Tanzania, and mounted three photographic exhibitions, participating, by the invitation of Italy's Ambassador to Tanzania, in a fourth. All four exhibitions were held in Dar es Salaam, the third being opened by the Rt. Hon. Zakia Meghji MP, Tanzania's Minister for Natural Resources and Tourism.

Many of his articles and photographs have appeared in wildlife and travel magazines, local and international.

About the Photographer

Javed Jafferji studied photography, film and television in the UK, before returning to Tanzania to publish over thirty books on East Africa. His work has been published in national and international newspapers and magazines. He has held exhibitions in London, Paris, Berlin and Pakistan as well as Tanzania.

Javed also publishes 'The Swahili Coast' magazine to promote eco-tourism in Tanzania and 'Tanzania Travel & Tourism Directory' the official tourism directory published in association with Tourism Confederation of Tanzania and Tanzania Tourist Board, He also manages a photography and graphic design company, and runs a shop, Zanzibar Gallery, which sells gifts, clothes, books and antiques.